embroidered home

To Barbs, for showing me this path and helping me stay on it.
To Garth, for your belief and confidence in my abilities.

embroidered home

Stitch stylish cushions, throws, napkins, bags and more

KELLY FLETCHER

Photography by Vanessa Davies

Kyle Books

CONTENTS

Introduction: Creative Surface

Embroidery	6
Embroidery basics	8
Tips and techniques	9
Stitch directory	12
Preparing and sewing your project	16

BOLD · 20

Pomegranate cushion	22
Pincushion	26
Picnic blanket strap	28
Birdhouse wall art	32
Stacked bowls tea towel	34
Bold motifs	36

COASTAL · 38

Coral cushion	40
Hanging fish	44
Nautical knot napkins	46
Beach bag	48
Wave towel tags	52
Coastal motifs	54

CONTEMPORARY · 56

Bird silhouette tote	58
Midnight wall art	62
Geometric laptop case	64
Abstract iPad sleeve	68
Cassette tape notebook	72
Contemporary motifs	75

COUNTRY 78

Cat doorstop	80
Leaf throw	84
Leaping hare chair pad	88
Gardening tool roll	90
Feather drawstring bag	94
Butterfly cosmetic bag	96
Country motifs	100

FLORAL 102

Dog rose Kindle cover	104
Summer bloom placemats	106
Growing wild wall art	110
Rambling pillowcases	113
Insect key fobs	116
Spring wreath	118
Floral motifs	120

VINTAGE 122

Needlebook	124
Bird coin purse	126
Glasses pouch	128
Radio hoop art	130
Kitchen scale apron	134
Vintage motifs	138

FESTIVE 140

Fair Isle reindeer runner	142
Snowflake stocking	146
Star garland	149
Holly cutlery holder	152
Hanging birds	154
Tree ornaments	156

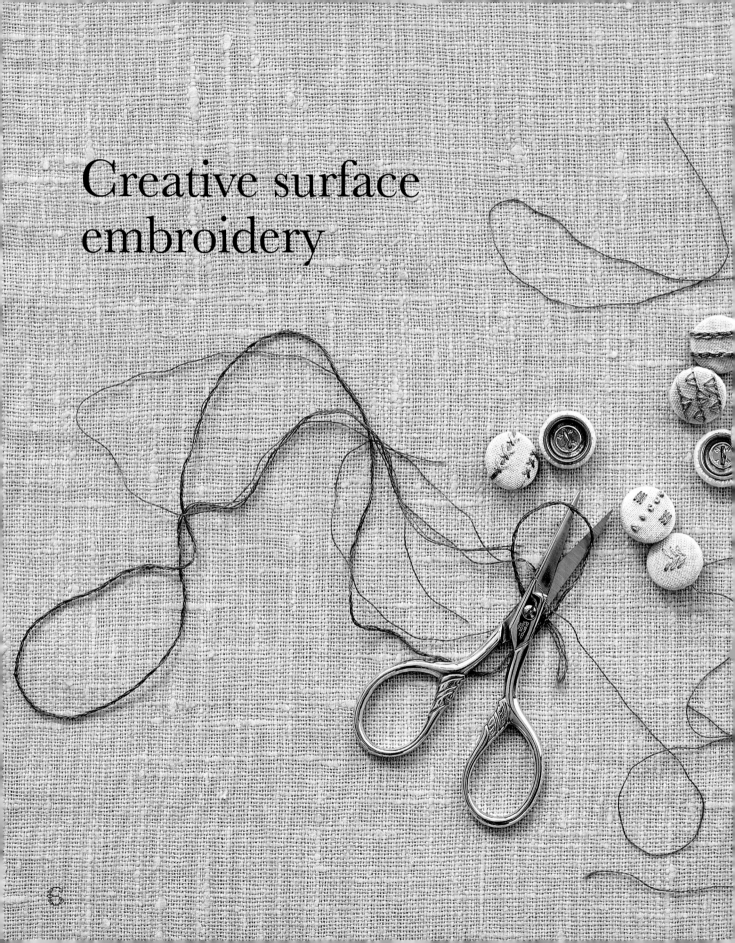

Creative surface embroidery

The style of embroidery used in this book is creative surface embroidery, which is all about the stitches. There are more than 200 different stitches, from everyday staples such as back and stem stitch, to more involved stitches such as whipped spider web and moss stitch. I've used 55 in this book, as they were the ones most suited to the designs, but you can always get creative and substitute them for others. The huge variety of stitches on offer is what makes this type of embroidery fun and interesting to do, and keeps you engaged in the stitching.

As important as neatness and a beautifully finished project are, enjoyment is ultimately the only thing that'll keep you embroidering. So although it's natural to want to strive for the best stitching possible, remember to focus, too, on the immensely pleasurable and tactile act of stitching by hand – that's the feeling that will keep you moving from one project to the next.

Instructions on how to do the stitches are given here, but the projects are the focus of this book, so the stitch directory is simple yet easy to understand. If you're a beginner, you might find it useful to go online and search for step-by-step photo and video stitch tutorials, of which there are many.

None of the projects in this book are beyond the skills of even beginner embroiderers, though. They are all design-based rather than overly dependent on stitch technique and with a little perseverance, anyone can make them.

Being largely self-taught, my approach is to do what works for me because innovation generally only comes with experimentation. I've studied every stitch book I have been able to get my hands on and from these it seems evident to me that embroidery stitch techniques, like everything in life, adapt and change over time. So take liberties with your stitching, because you never know what the outcome may be.

Lastly, your home should reflect who you are. So if you're an embroiderer or sewist, it should be full of the things you've whiled away the hours embroidering and sewing. If this is not the case, hopefully this book will see you well on your way.

Embroidery basics

SUPPLIES

Needles

Embroidery needles are sometimes called crewel needles and have a large eye to make them easier to thread. Size 7 needles are good for working three to six strands, size 8 for two to three strands and size 9 for one to three strands of thread.

Milliners are also known as straw needles. They're used for working knots, bullions and cast-on stitches, and stitches such as pistil that have a knot element. They're the same width from eye to tip, allowing the thread to pull easily through the wrapped thread that becomes the knot.

Thread

The projects in this book are embroidered in DMC six-stranded cotton. It's widely available and versatile as it can be split into strands to achieve various thicknesses. It comes in a variety of colours and is relatively inexpensive, so you can build up a stash.

The six strands are twisted into one thread, which you'll have to split according to the embroidery instructions for each project. Cut a length of thread, generally about 50cm. Divide it into the number of strands you need at one end, then slide a finger between the strands and down the length of the thread to separate them.

You can stitch with the thread as it is or separate it further into single strands and then regroup them. I let the stitch determine which I do, separating the thread into individual strands for stitches where twists in the thread will show (blanket, satin and straight stitch) and leaving them as is where visually it won't really make a difference (stem and chain stitch). Separating the strands gives the stitches a smoother look as the strands lie neatly alongside one another.

While six-stranded thread has a natural twist to it, it can become too twisted as you work and leave your stitches looking thin and scraggly. When this starts to happen, either spin your needle between your thumb and forefinger to untwist the thread a bit or turn your hoop upside down and let your needle dangle – the thread will untwist naturally.

Embroidery scissors

A small pair of scissors with fine, sharp points is best for embroidery. You can buy specialist embroidery scissors, but any sharp pair will do for cutting threads. Small scissors are easier to handle than bigger sewing scissors as the work you're doing is much finer. Sharp tips make it easier to snip the right thread and are helpful when unpicking stitches.

Hoops

Although not essential, an embroidery hoop will keep your fabric taut and help prevent it puckering as you stitch. Use a hoop just big enough for you to hold comfortably and move it around on the fabric as you embroider – you need to be able to work the stitches with relative ease to get good results. This type of embroidery will survive a bit of squashing – just pinch it back into place afterwards (but try to avoid squashing knots if you can help it, rather leave them until last).

I use mostly a 10cm (4-inch) hoop, sometimes a 12cm (5-inch), and I prefer beechwood hoops. If you use a wooden hoop, a handy trick is to keep a small screwdriver with your embroidery supplies and use that to tighten and loosen the outer ring – it saves your fingers and allows you to tighten the outer hoop more than you're able to by hand.

Remove the hoop from your fabric between stitching sessions to prevent it leaving permanent marks or creases in the fabric.

Thimbles

Using a thimble is down to personal preference. Traditional thimbles come in mainly metal, plastic and leather, or there are also stick-on thimble pads (from quilting shops) that have an adhesive back and will stick to the area of your finger that needs protecting.

Seam ripper

Also known as a quick unpick, a seam ripper is useful for unpicking embroidery. It has to be a sharp, good-quality one, though, otherwise it'll pull the threads instead of slicing through them and in the process pucker your work.

TIPS AND TECHNIQUES

Light

Try to embroider in good, natural light – your stitching will automatically be neater and you will put less strain on your eyes than doing it in low-level light. A lamp with a daylight bulb is a good alternative; a specialist daylight lamp is even better.

Ergonomics

Look after your eyesight, back, neck and hands while you are stitching. Surface embroidery is easier to do when you're able to rest your hoop hand against

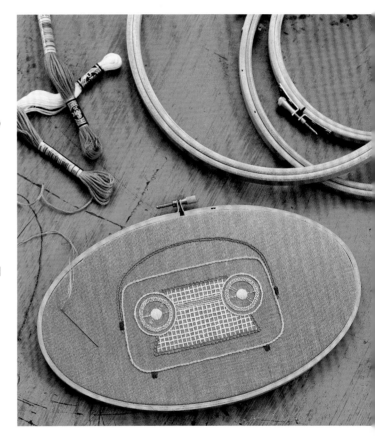

something, so sit either at a table or with a plump cushion on your lap. Regularly adjust your sitting position and get up every now and then to stretch. Shake your hands and flex your fingers every now and then, too. It's easy to get caught up in your work and stitch in the same position for hours.

Look up from your work at regular intervals and focus on something in the distance to relax your eyes. If you wear glasses, be sure to take some embroidery to the optometrist next time you have your eyes tested, it makes such a difference if your glasses are suited to stitching.

As soon as you start pricking your fingers repeatedly or feeling in the least bit frustrated, it's time to stop. Put your embroidery down, even if you're halfway through a row of stitching – it usually means you've done enough for the day.

Tension, stitch length, knots and unpicking

Tension is important as it influences how your embroidery will turn out; stitches pulled too tightly pucker the underlying fabric and those worked too loosely create loops on the surface of the fabric. The obvious advice is simply practice. I would suggest that you focus on one stitch at a time, especially when learning a new stitch.

Take your time over each individual stitch in the row, make it as neatly and as evenly as you can and allow your instinct to determine the stitch size. It'll be easier to settle into your natural rhythm and a good tension should follow automatically. Everyone's instinctive stitch size and tension is different and once you get the hang of yours, you can begin experimenting with stitching against your natural inclination to get different results.

Knots are the bane of an embroiderer's life, but they happen. Use a needle to get between the strands of a knot – two if necessary – and work them loose. But don't waste too much time undoing knots, rather cut your losses and start a new strand of thread if you encounter a particularly stubborn one.

Accept that unpicking is part of embroidering. It's better to go back a stitch or two straight away than get to the end and have one bad stitch ruining an otherwise good row.

Storing your work

Cover your embroidery when not working on it to keep it clean and out of harm's way. Remove the hoop when you're done for the day and fold up the piece of embroidery neatly, folding in the edges rather than folding the fabric down the middle of the design where possible. Store your project in a tote bag or wrapped in a piece of fabric (a project wrap).

Left-handers

Left-handed embroiderers naturally stitch in the opposite direction to those of us who are right-handed, generally creating stitches that are mirror images of the ones found in stitch books. If you are left-handed and struggle to flip the stitches in your mind, a basic solution is to hold the instructions up to a mirror. If you plan to do a fair amount of embroidery, though, it might be an idea to invest in

a stitch book or build up a catalogue of online tutorials for left-handed embroiderers.

STARTING AND ENDING THREADS

Threads need to be secured so your embroidery doesn't come undone. Here are some methods:

- **Double stitch to start:** If you've backed your fabric with cotton voile (which I recommend – see page 18), start with a small double stitch through the voile only and under the area or line you're about to embroider so it doesn't show through if your fabric is light in colour.

- **Knot to start:** There is always going to be debate around knots – the main reason to avoid using one is if it's going to create a visible bump. You're not going to see this if you're filling in an area with knots, but you might if you're stitching an outline in a flat stitch such as back stitch.

- **Waste knot to start:** Knot the end of your thread and take it down through the fabric a few centimetres from your start point. Snip the knot off when you're done and weave the thread through the back of your stitching to secure it.

- **Knot to end:** Make a knot in your thread if you don't think threading it away will secure it well enough or if it's not going to show through the fabric, such as behind knots or an area filled with padded satin or circular Rhodes stitch. Thread your needle through a loop in the thread and guide the knot down to the surface of the fabric before pulling it tight.

HOW TO READ THE EMBROIDERY INSTRUCTIONS

The embroidery instructions for each of the designs are given as diagrams. The key for these instructions is as follows:

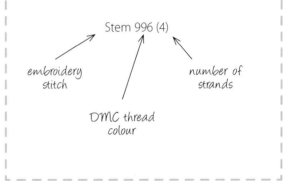

Stem 996 (4)

embroidery stitch

number of strands

DMC thread colour

- **Whipping/lacing to end:** This is the easiest way to secure your thread. Take it to the back of the fabric and either whip or lace it back along the row of stitching you've just completed for a little way, until you're sure the thread won't come loose.

- **Trimming threads:** When you've secured your thread at the end of a row of stitching, cut away the excess so you aren't left with 'tails' on the back of your embroidery. They'll get caught up in subsequent stitching (sometimes pulling through to the front) and show through if you're working on light-coloured fabric. Trimming means the back of your work will look a lot neater, too.

Stitch directory
55 SURFACE EMBROIDERY STITCHES

Arrowhead stitch

Running stitch

Straight stitch

Back stitch

Back stitch – trellis

Long and short stitch

Satin stitch

Satin stitch – padded

Seeding – double

Stem stitch

Chain stitch – cable

Chain stitch – detached

Chain stitch – heavy

Chain stitch – twisted

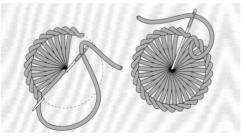

Blanket stitch – pinwheel closed

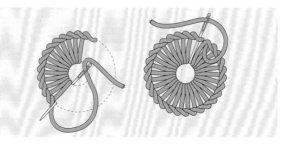

Blanket stitch – pinwheel open

Blanket stitch – partial pinwheel

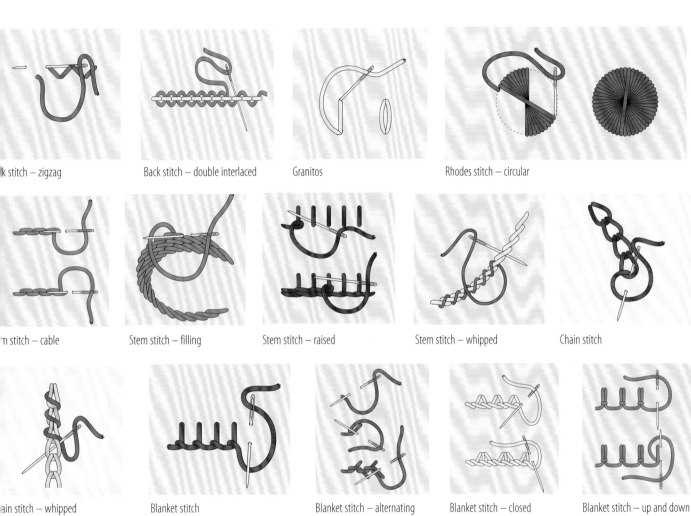

k stitch – zigzag

Back stitch – double interlaced

Granitos

Rhodes stitch – circular

m stitch – cable

Stem stitch – filling

Stem stitch – raised

Stem stitch – whipped

Chain stitch

ain stitch – whipped

Blanket stitch

Blanket stitch – alternating

Blanket stitch – closed

Blanket stitch – up and down

eather stitch

Feather stitch – double

Feather stitch – long-armed

Fly stitch

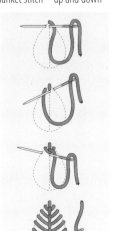

Fly stitch – leaf

 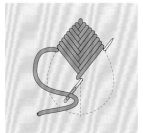  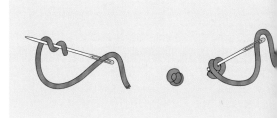

Cross stitch

Cross stitch – double

Fishbone stitch

Moss stitch

 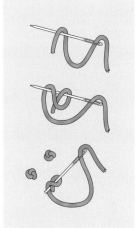  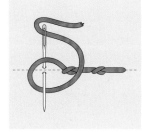 

Chinese knot

Colonial knot

Coral stitch

French knot (the French knots in this book are made by wrapping the thread around the needle twice, unless otherwise indicated)

 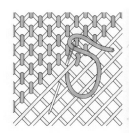

Pistil stitch

Wheatear stitch

Couching

Couching - trellis

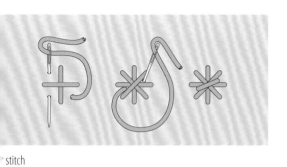

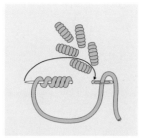

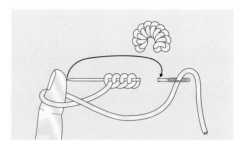

stitch

Bullion knot

Cast-on stitch

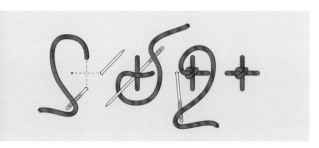

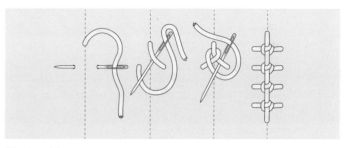

-legged knot

Palestrina stitch

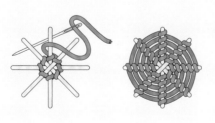

Spider web – whipped

af filling stitch

Preparing and sewing your project

All the projects in this book start off the same way, with a design transferred onto fabric. So the preparation required before you start embroidering is the same for each project.

1. FABRIC

I recommend you use natural fabrics with a close weave. This is your foundation fabric – the fabric you will embellish with embroidery. Choose cottons, linens or blends of the two that have a smooth finish and aren't too thick. I use a lot of quilters' cotton for my projects as it's a good weight for hand stitching, has minimal stretch and comes in a variety of colours.

As a general rule, always pre-wash your fabric. This not only gets rid of dust or marks (lighter fabrics), but it also draws out any excess dye (darker fabrics). More importantly, though, any shrinkage that is going to occur in the fabric will happen during pre-washing rather than once embroidered.

Dissolve some washing powder or liquid detergent in a basin of tepid water. The temperature will draw the excess dye out of the fabric more easily and encourage any shrinking. Wash the fabric thoroughly by hand and rinse it in cold water to remove the detergent. Hang the fabric and allow it to drip dry. If you have a large piece of fabric or several pieces of a similar shade (all light, or all dark), you can machine wash it with the temperature set to 30°C and then hang it to dry. You may want to overlock or zigzag the raw edges first to prevent the fabric unravelling.

Once dry, steam-iron the fabric, spraying it with water to remove any stubborn creases. This will force the last of any shrinking, plus beautifully smooth fabric is essential for neat design transfer.

Cutting your fabric

The cutting measurements for each project are given in centimetres, with an inches conversion in brackets.

I often work in inches, simply because I use a rotary cutter, cutting mat and quilting rulers. These save time and give me greater accuracy when cutting. But for bigger projects, such as the table runner or tote bag, I use a tape measure in conjunction with the rulers to draw elements such as cutting lines onto the fabric. A good pair of sewing scissors is essential for any non-linear cutting.

2. TRANSFERRING THE DESIGN

This is a crucial step, as an accurately transferred design automatically leads to neater embroidery and leaves you free to enjoy the stitching process rather than struggling to embroider a straight line. Transferring a design onto well-ironed fabric is a start, but your method of transfer and choice of transfer tools will also affect accuracy.

Choose the transfer method that best suits your fabric: white dressmakers' carbon works well on dark fabric, pencil is good for white or light fabric, and iron-on transfers make it easier to transfer a design onto a fabric with a bit of texture. Test the methods to find out which one works for you.

Generally, it's best to use pencils, pens and fabric markers with sharp/fine points as they create a thinner line that's more precise and easier to cover with embroidery. And look out for stencils and rulers that'll help you transfer designs more accurately – I have a stencil of various-sized circles and two clear rulers of different lengths that I find invaluable.

Sometimes it's necessary to touch up your design as you embroider. There are lots of fabric markers on the market in addition to a basic 2B pencil; you're looking for those with a sharp point that won't bleed into the fabric and that can be removed afterwards without damaging the embroidery. Haberdasheries and quilt shops usually have good options, as well as specialist embroidery stores.

The embroidery patterns for the projects in this book are given at full size or with percentages for enlarging them, and once at full size, are the optimal size for the corresponding embroidery instructions. If you'd like to reduce or enlarge a design, it's more than likely you'll have to adapt the embroidery instructions as well. First check that the recommended stitches will work at the new scale and replace those that won't, then adjust the number of strands of thread up or down in line with the new size of the design.

Three ways to transfer designs onto fabric

Trace using a 2B pencil:
A 2B pencil has soft lead, which is easier to wash out of fabric than harder leads. But it's still better to cover all drawn lines with stitching, so take care when tracing a design onto fabric and keep your pencil point sharp or use a clutch pencil for a fine line.

- Tape the design to your light box or a window – choose a window where you can stand or sit at a comfortable height, and one which is away from direct sunlight to make it easier on your eyes.

3M Scotch Magic Tape 810 works well as it peels off again easily without leaving marks on fabric, as does masking tape.
- Tape your fabric over the paper printout, positioning the design where you want it, and trace it onto the fabric.

Transfer using dressmakers' carbon:
This is a particularly good method to use if you're transferring the design onto dark fabric (use white dressmakers' carbon) or a solid-coloured fabric (use contrasting carbon).

- Tape your fabric to your work surface (see note on tape above).
- Position the design where you want it and tape the top edge to your fabric.
- Flip the design up and place a piece of dressmakers' carbon face down under it, then flip it back down and draw over the lines. Use a fine-tipped pen and firm pressure on a fairly hard work surface to get the best results.

Transfer using an iron-on transfer pencil:
Iron-on transfers allow you to transfer an image or outlines onto fabric using a hot iron. It's best to read the manufacturer's instructions first, as well as the stitch instructions, to make sure all the lines will be covered with embroidery (they will not wash out), before you iron the design onto your fabric.

- Use the design in reverse (so it will appear the right way round once ironed onto the fabric). Copy it onto a piece of paper and then flip it over and draw over the lines on the back, or scan it and flip it using image software – you want a mirror image of the original.
- Trace the design onto tracing paper with the iron-on transfer pencil. Trim away the excess to make positioning easier. The design should transfer several times onto 100 per cent cotton or other natural fabric.
- Place the design face down on your fabric and press firmly with a dry iron for 5–10 seconds. Try not to slide the iron, rather lift it gently and reposition it. Lift a corner of the transfer to check that the design has transferred to the fabric before lifting it off completely.

using light or dark fabric. Buy a few metres at a time so you always have some on hand.

Being a natural fibre, cotton voile is prone to shrinking. Give it the same treatment as your foundation fabric in terms of washing and ironing before using it as backing in a project.

4. PREPARING YOUR EMBROIDERY FOR SEWING

A steam iron is essential for removing creases, hoop marks and folds. Once the embroidery is complete, iron it face down on a towel. This will prevent the embroidery being ironed flat as the stitching will sink into the pile of the towel. You can press quite firmly with this type of embroidery as six-stranded cotton is fairly robust, as is the usually cotton or linen foundation fabric.

Sewing supplies

You'll need some basic sewing supplies to make the projects in this book:

- Sewing machine with zipper foot
- Overlocker (optional)
- Fabric/sewing scissors
- Sewing pins
- Tape measure
- Cutting mat (optional)
- Quilters' ruler/s (optional)
- Rotary cutter (optional)
- Iron, with steam setting
- Ironing board
- Fabric markers
- Sharp needles (for general hand sewing)

- Generally, the longer you iron, the darker the transfer. The ink may fade with washing, but this is not guaranteed.

3. BACKING YOUR FOUNDATION FABRIC

Attaching a piece of cotton voile or finely woven muslin fabric to the back of your work helps stabilise the stitching and gives you somewhere to secure your thread when starting a new row or section. It also helps prevent your fabric from puckering or pulling too much as you embroider.

Cut a piece of voile the same size as your foundation fabric and tack, overlock or stitch it to the back by machine with a zigzag stitch. If the design is only on a small section of the fabric, tack a square of voile or muslin behind the design and trim the excess away once you've finished the embroidery.

Some projects, such as napkins, don't look good with backing fabric. But otherwise I back everything with cotton voile. It's not overly expensive and comes in a variety of colours so you can match it to your foundation fabric. I tend to use white voile because it doesn't show through, irrespective of whether you're

Fabric and materials

Use fabric that is similar or well suited to the fabric on which you've embroidered, to make the project easier to sew. Sticking with natural fibres eliminates a lot of those that are trickier to sew, but otherwise try to avoid fabric that unravels easily or has too much stretch in it.

Invest in the best-quality fabrics and materials you can afford. There's nothing worse than spending hours and hours hand embroidering something only to have the end result flop because of inferior materials. This goes for everything from fabric and threads to zips and cord to batting and stiffening.

5. SEWING

The instructions for making up the finished items in this book are as basic as I could make them. I've tried to work out the straightest line to get from embellished cloth to practical item for the home to keep things simple on the sewing front. Seams are hidden inside inner and outer layers wherever possible and hand stitching creates neat finishes. You are, of course, free to adapt, adjust and alter the patterns according to your skill with a machine and to suit your taste and needs.

CARING FOR YOUR EMBROIDERY

Sometimes it's necessary to wash the finished embroidery: hoops may have left marks, mysterious smudges may have appeared on the fabric and traced-on lines may still be showing. The main thing to try to avoid is your threads running and the colour seeping into the surrounding fabric – red threads in particular are the ones to watch out for here. If possible, spot clean the embroidery rather than wash the whole piece of fabric.

The best way to wash your embroidery is by hand. Dissolve your detergent or powder in cold water and submerge the embroidery while keeping it as flat as possible. For stubborn marks in the fabric, make a paste with a little washing powder and rub it into the affected area (avoid using the multi-coloured stain remover granules as they can bleed colour into the fabric). Try not to rub too hard or too much as the fabric may pill. Rinse the embroidery well to remove all traces of detergent and allow it to drip dry – smooth the fabric out well while it's still wet. Iron the embroidery when it's almost dry, face down on a towel to avoid squashing the stitching.

Threads are unlikely to run after the first hand wash, so household items embellished with creative surface embroidery in six-stranded cotton can be washed with the everyday laundry thereafter. Smooth the item out well when hanging it to dry and continue ironing it face down on a towel, and your embroidery should look good for ages, even after several washes.

bold

*Light-hearted splashes of interest
inspired by Scandinavian design and
nature*

Fabric

- 0.5m (20 inches) white cotton
- 1m (40 inches) white cotton voile backing fabric
- 0.5m (20 inches) aubergine cotton
- 744 Pale yellow
- 902 Very dark garnet

Thread

DMC six-stranded cotton thread:

- 907 Light parrot green
- B5200 Snow white
- 3802 Very dark antique mauve
- 315 Medium dark antique mauve
- 743 Medium yellow

Needles

- Embroidery: size 7, 9
- Milliner: size 5, 7, 8

Other

- 35cm (14 inch) zip, white
- Stuffing
- Matching sewing thread

The rich aubergine, deep yellow and uplifting green embroidery gives the cushion a classic feel, but juicy pinks and fresh lemon yellow threads would work just as well.

Pomegranate cushion

QUIRK UP YOUR COUCH WITH A FRUITY PILLOW

The open blanket stitch pinwheels that give each pomegranate seed its shape lend uniformity to the design, while the variety of stitches inside each seed keeps things interesting and engaging. Avoid squashing knots in your hoop by stitching them last, before you move on to the next section of seeds.

This is technically a box cushion but one that is made to fit a custom-shaped inner – in this case a pomegranate. The boxing or fabric inset that makes up the sides of the cushion can be a little tricky to sew but it is well worth the effort as it adds a splash of colour that enhances the embroidery and allows the cushion to keep its shape to better display the stitching. It's perfectly doable if you take your time and do a little tacking before stitching by machine.

prepare

- Cut a 50 x 50cm (20 x 20 inch) piece of white cotton and a 50 x 50cm (20 x 20 inch) piece of cotton voile.

transfer

- Transfer the embroidery design onto the white cotton using one of the methods on page 17. Include the cutting lines. Overlock or tack the voile to the back of the fabric.

embroider

- Embroider the design according to the instructions.
- Iron the finished embroidery when you're done by placing it face down on a towel and ironing the back of the work.

cut

- Check that the traced-on cutting lines haven't distorted during stitching and redraw them if necessary, then cut out the embroidered cushion front.
- Use the templates provided to cut out the two back panels.
- For the cushion inset, cut 4.5cm (1¾ inch) wide strips of the aubergine cotton on the cross. Join until you have a 153cm (60 inch) strip.
- For the cushion inner, use the cutting lines of the design for the cushion front as a template, but add a 0.6cm (¼ inch) seam allowance, and cut two pomegranate shapes from the remaining cotton voile. Fold the fabric in half and cut both at the same time, so one is a mirror image of the other. Create a 153cm (60 inch) strip, cut on the cross, in the same way as for the cushion cover from the remaining cotton voile.

Front template and embroidery design
Enlarge by 500%

Back templates
Enlarge by 500%

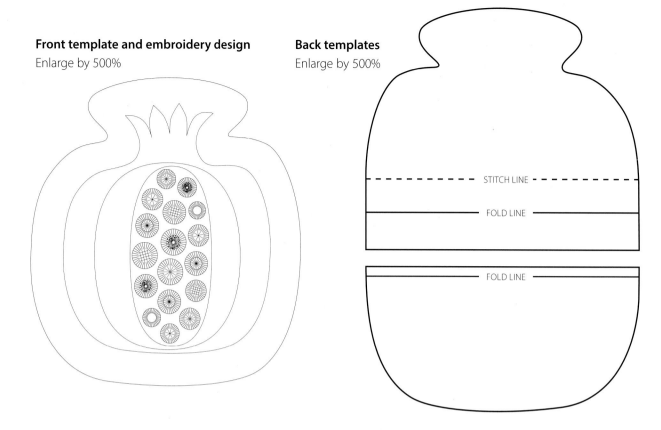

STITCH LINE

FOLD LINE

FOLD LINE

sew

- Overlock or zigzag the zip edges of each panel, then iron a 1.2cm (½ inch) hem into the lower back piece of fabric and a 5cm (2 inch) hem into the upper back piece. Using a suitable fabric marker, draw a line across the width of the upper piece of fabric, 4.5cm (1¾ inches) above the fold.

- Insert the zip: Place the zip face down and centred on the top edge of the smaller piece of fabric. Tack it in place, keeping the zip's teeth just below the ironed fold line. Stitch by machine along the fold line, using a zipper foot. Fold the ironed turnover back again so that the zip flips and is facing upwards/right side up. Position the upper piece of the cushion back so that the 5cm (2 inch) fold overlaps the lower piece by 4cm (1½ inches) (lay the two pieces on top of the cushion front at this stage to check for size and adjust the overlap if necessary). Tack the upper edge of the zip to the top piece of the cushion back and topstitch across the entire width – along the drawn line – using the zipper foot. Remove the line with a damp cloth or as advised by the fabric marker manufacturer.

- Pin the aubergine strip to the front of the cushion, right sides facing, and stitch in place using a 0.6cm (¼ inch) seam.

- Open the zip in the cushion back about halfway and pin the back of the cushion to the aubergine strip. Sew the two together, again using a 0.6cm (¼ inch) seam.

- Turn the cushion the right way round through the zip opening, push out the corners and press the seams.

- Make the cushion inner the same way as the cover, but without the zip. Instead, leave a gap along one edge, turn the cushion inner the right way around, stuff it and then stitch the gap closed by hand. Use a 0.6cm (¼ inch) seam. Insert the stuffed inner into the cushion cover to finish.

For a firmer cushion, pad out the body of the pomegranate using the upholstery trick of wrapping the main section of the cushion inner in batting – quilters' batting works well – and cobbling it in place.

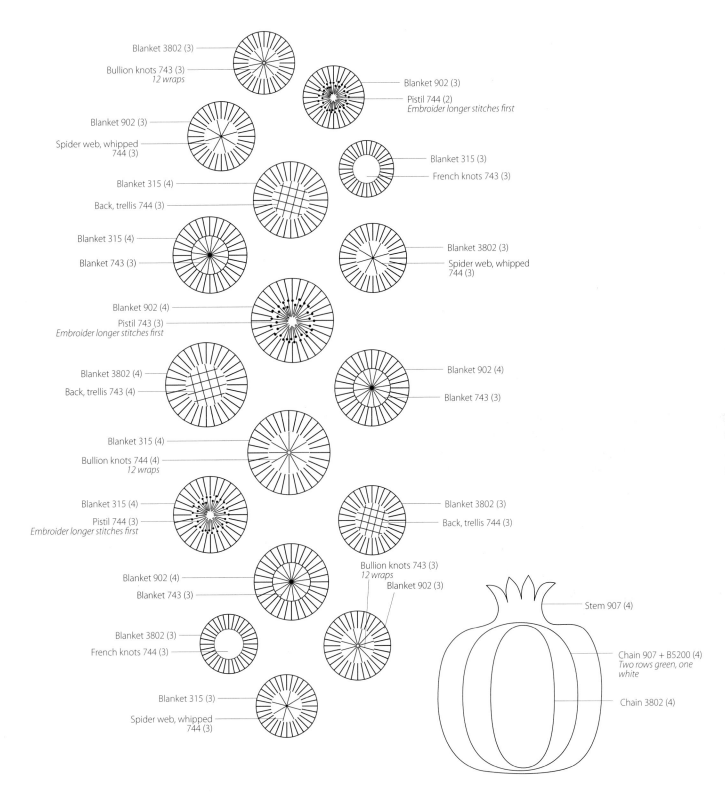

Blanket 3802 (3)

Bullion knots 743 (3)
12 wraps

Blanket 902 (3)

Pistil 744 (2)
Embroider longer stitches first

Blanket 902 (3)

Spider web, whipped
744 (3)

Blanket 315 (3)

French knots 743 (3)

Blanket 315 (4)

Back, trellis 744 (3)

Blanket 315 (4)

Blanket 743 (3)

Blanket 3802 (3)

Spider web, whipped
744 (3)

Blanket 902 (4)

Pistil 743 (3)
Embroider longer stitches first

Blanket 3802 (4)

Back, trellis 743 (4)

Blanket 902 (4)

Blanket 743 (3)

Blanket 315 (4)

Bullion knots 744 (4)
12 wraps

Blanket 315 (4)

Pistil 744 (3)
Embroider longer stitches first

Blanket 3802 (3)

Back, trellis 744 (3)

Blanket 902 (4)

Blanket 743 (3)

Bullion knots 743 (3)
12 wraps

Blanket 902 (3)

Stem 907 (4)

Blanket 3802 (3)

French knots 744 (3)

Chain 907 + B5200 (4)
*Two rows green, one
white*

Chain 3802 (4)

Blanket 315 (3)

Spider web, whipped
744 (3)

Pincushion

A SPLASH OF COLOUR FOR YOUR SEWING TABLE

A symmetrical border of leaves and knots leave the centre of this handy pincushion clear for pins and needles.

Make a few of these pincushions in different colours to keep your appliqué pins separate from your sewing pins and your embroidery needles apart from your hand sewing needles. Or give them to your stitching friends as gifts. Pincushions are great for using up scraps of your most favourite or precious fabric, as you'll probably use them for years to come.

Fabric
- 20 x 25cm (7 x 9 inches) white cotton
- 20 x 25cm (7 x 9 inches) white cotton voile backing fabric
- 10 x 15cm (4 x 6 inches) green cotton

Thread
DMC six-stranded cotton thread:
- 907 Light parrot green
- 743 Medium yellow

Needles
- Embroidery: size 7
- Milliner: size 7

Other
- Stuffing
- Matching sewing thread

Use the weave of the fabric as a guide to keep your knots in a straight row.

Embroidery instructions and design

Full size

French knots 743 (3)
Detached chain 907 (3)
Stem 907 (3)

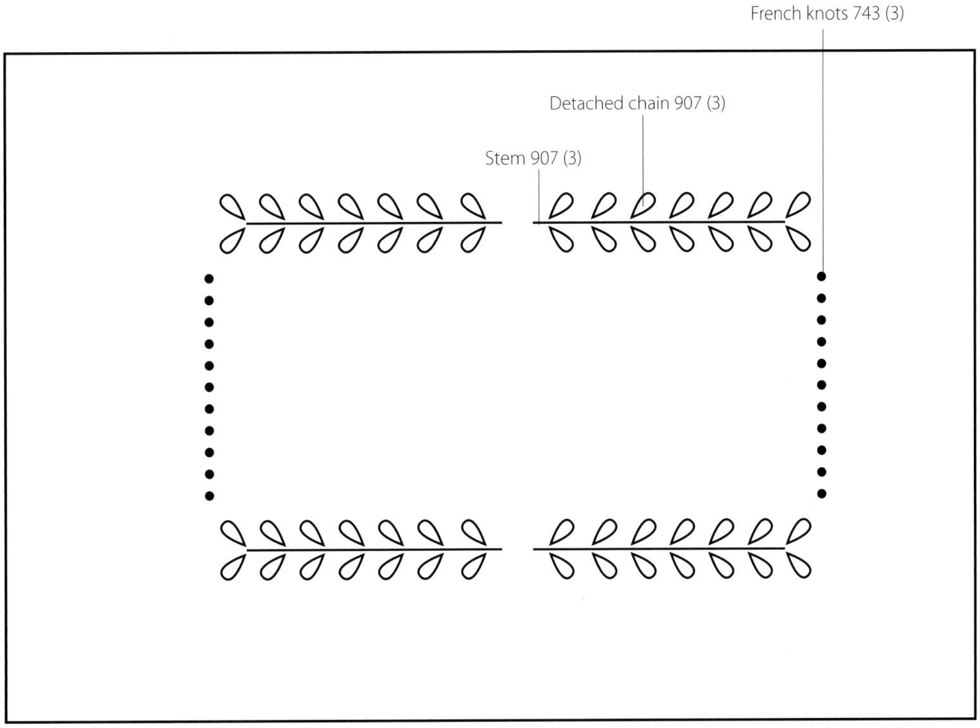

transfer

- Transfer the embroidery design onto the white cotton using one of the methods given on page 17. Include the cutting lines. Overlock or tack the voile to the back of the fabric.

embroider

- Embroider the design according to the instructions.
- Place the completed embroidery face down on a towel and iron the back.

cut

- Check that the traced-on cutting lines haven't distorted during stitching and redraw them if necessary before cutting out the pincushion.
- Cut a 9 x 13.5cm (3½ x 5¼ inch) rectangle of green cotton.

sew

- Iron a 1.2cm (½ inch) hem into the shorter side of the pincushion with excess fabric. Do the same to one of the shorter sides of the pincushion back. This makes it easier to stitch the pincushion closed once it's stuffed.
- Join the embroidered front to the back using a 0.6cm (¼ inch) seam with right sides facing. Stitch around three sides, leaving the one with the pressed seam open.
- Trim the corners and turn the pincushion the right way round. Push the corners out neatly with a closed pair of sewing scissors or other suitable tool.
- Press the seams and stuff the pincushion, then stitch the open end closed by hand along the ironed fold lines.

Black and white patterned fabric will offset any bright, solid-coloured fabric and stitching well.

Picnic blanket strap

A FIELD OF FLOWERS FROM A FAVOURED FEASTING SPOT

The various elements that make up this design have been arranged to fit around the practical aspects of a blanket strap – such as the handle – and still look good when rolled around a picnic blanket. The flowers, sprigs, leaves and pods are fairly stylised, making it easier to get away with unconventional colour choices such as red leaves and blue flowers.

Slide buckles secure the blanket strap, eliminating the need to make holes in the straps – a simple fabric strap is sufficient. And wrapping the backing fabric around the edges of the embroidered panel brings additional colour to front of the strap as well as being an easy way to back the embroidery. Thick stiffening gives the fabric enough substance to allow the blanket strap to keep its shape.

Fabric
- 30cm (12 inches) white cotton
- 70 x 30cm (28 x 12 inches) white cotton voile backing fabric
- 30cm (12 inches) black and white checked cotton
- 10cm (4 inches) bright yellow cotton (110cm/43 inches) wide

Thread
DMC six-stranded cotton thread:
- 744 Pale yellow
- 743 Medium yellow
- 907 Light parrot green
- 964 Light sea green
- B5200 Snow white
- 169 Light pewter
- 168 Very light pewter
- 351 Coral
- 350 Medium coral
- 347 Very dark salmon
- 796 Dark royal blue
- 798 Dark Delft blue

Needles
- Embroidery: size 7, 9
- Milliner: size 5, 7, 8

Other
- Two slide buckles, 20mm (¾ inch) wide
- Medium-weight iron-on stiffening (Vilene)
- Yellow and white thread, or other matching sewing thread

prepare

- Draw a 66 x 23cm (26 x 9 inch) rectangle onto the white cotton fabric.

transfer

- Centre the embroidery design inside the drawn-on rectangle and transfer using one of the methods given on page 17. Overlock or tack the voile to the back of the fabric.

embroider

- Embroider the design according to the instructions.
- Iron the embroidered fabric face down on a towel when complete.

cut

- Check that the drawn-on cutting lines haven't distorted during stitching and redraw them if necessary before cutting out the embroidered front of the blanket strap.
- Cut a 74 x 30.5cm (29 x 12 inch) rectangle of black and white cotton.
- Cut a 66 x 23cm (26 x 9 inch) rectangle of stiffening.
- Cut a 19 x 8cm (7½ x 3 inch) rectangle of black and white cotton for the handle.
- Cut a 5cm (2 inch) strip of yellow cotton, the width of the fabric.

sew

- Fuse the stiffening to the back of the embroidered panel. Iron with the embroidery face down on a towel.
- Position the embroidered panel in the centre of the black and white fabric with wrong sides facing and fold a 2cm (¾ inch) double-fold hem over the embroidered front on all four sides. Mitre the corners and pin in place before machine stitching all the way round the panel, joining the back to the front.
- Stitch the black and white handle in half lengthways with right sides facing using a 0.6cm (¼ inch) seam. Press the seam open and turn the right way round (attaching a safety pin to one end and then passing it through the tube is an easy way to do this). Position the seam down the centre and press the handle flat. Iron a 0.6cm (¼ inch) hem into either end of the handle so the seam is on the underside and position it where shown on the embroidered panel, so the ends are 4cm (1½ inches) from the edge. The strap has some give – it doesn't lie flat. Stitch in place with two rows of stitching at each end, 0.6cm (¼ inch) and 1cm (⅜ inch) from the edge – the second row of stitching hides the raw edges of the handle.

- Use yellow thread on the top and white thread on the bobbin (or suitable matching colours) when attaching the straps.
- Cut a 52cm (20½ inch) piece from the strip of yellow cotton for the straps. Stitch a 1.2cm (½ inch) hem into either end and then stitch in half lengthways with a 0.6cm (¼ inch) seam. Press the seam open and turn the right way round (use a safety pin to do this). Position the seam so it runs down the centre of the strip and press flat. Then cut it in half so you have two pieces, each 26cm (10¼ inch) in length. Stitch the hemmed ends closed with a second row of stitching, 0.6cm (¼ inch) from the first. Fold a 1.5cm (⅝ inch) hem into the other end of each strap and press, then position each strap on one end of the blanket strap so the folded hem lies 6.5cm (2⅝ inches) from the top edge and 4cm (1½ inches) from the sides. Stitch a 2cm (¾ inch) square with a cross inside it over the folded fabric for strength, pivoting the fabric with your needle in the down position at the corners.
- Fold the remainder of the yellow cotton strip in half and stitch lengthways using a 0.6cm (¼ inch) seam. Cut two 13.5cm (5¼ inch) pieces for the buckle straps. Fold each strip in half and thread the buckle onto it (over the centre bar), then fold both ends together to create a 1.5cm (⅝ inch) hem and press in place. Attach the buckle straps to the other side of the blanket strap, positioning them so the folded hem lies 12cm (4⅝inches) from the lower edge and 4cm (1½ inches) from the sides. Stitch a square with a cross inside it over the folded fabric for strength, pivoting the fabric with your needle in the down position at the corners and catching the raw edges of the strap fabric inside the stitching.
- Wrap the blanket strap around a rolled-up blanket and tighten in place by threading the straps through the buckles.

Opt for wider stitches such as chain stitch when embroidering with white thread on white fabric – they'll be more visible.

Embroidery instructions and design

Enlarge by 200%

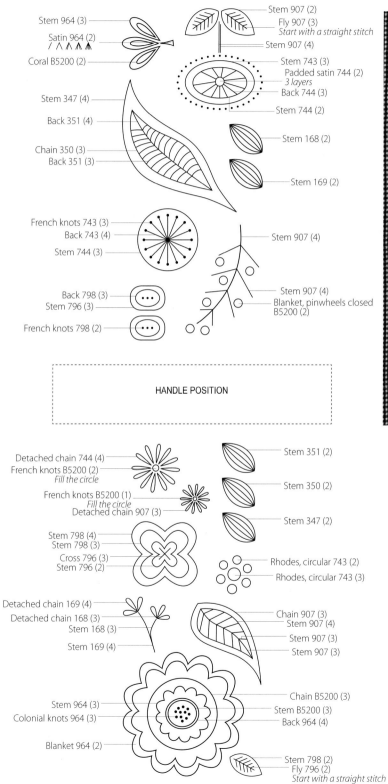

Stem 964 (3)
Satin 964 (2)
Coral B5200 (2)

Stem 907 (2)
Fly 907 (3)
Start with a straight stitch
Stem 907 (4)

Stem 347 (4)
Back 351 (4)

Chain 350 (3)
Back 351 (3)

Stem 743 (3)
Padded satin 744 (2)
3 layers
Back 744 (3)
Stem 744 (2)

Stem 168 (2)

Stem 169 (2)

French knots 743 (3)
Back 743 (4)
Stem 744 (3)

Stem 907 (4)

Back 798 (3)
Stem 796 (3)

French knots 798 (2)

Stem 907 (4)
Blanket, pinwheels closed
B5200 (2)

HANDLE POSITION

Detached chain 744 (4)
French knots B5200 (2)
Fill the circle

French knots B5200 (1)
Fill the circle
Detached chain 907 (3)

Stem 798 (4)
Stem 798 (3)
Cross 796 (3)
Stem 796 (2)

Detached chain 169 (4)
Detached chain 168 (3)
Stem 168 (3)
Stem 169 (4)

Stem 351 (2)

Stem 350 (2)

Stem 347 (2)

Rhodes, circular 743 (2)
Rhodes, circular 743 (3)

Chain 907 (3)
Stem 907 (4)
Stem 907 (3)
Stem 907 (3)

Stem 964 (3)
Colonial knots 964 (3)

Blanket 964 (2)

Chain B5200 (3)
Stem B5200 (3)
Back 964 (4)

Stem 798 (2)
Fly 796 (2)
Start with a straight stitch

Birdhouse wall art

THE HOMES OF BIRDS TO ADORN YOUR HOME

The roofs make this design; filled with textured and sometimes unusual stitches, they ground the design, making it possible to incorporate white on white embroidery. Think through the stitching on the roofs before beginning: plan the direction of your satin stitching, evenly space the foundation straight stitches for the raised stem stitch roof, decide where to place your rows of chain stitch to keep the roof edges smooth and work out how your rows of raised stem, chain, closed blanket and twisted chain are going to meet up at the apex.

The irregular shape of the design means you're probably going to have to get a frame for this made to size. If you do go down the professional route, ask your framer to use non-reflective glass so your embroidery is more visible.

Using a substantial number of strands of white thread on the white background fabric improves the visibility of the stem-stitched outline of the birdhouses.

Play around with the spacing of the uprights when doing blanket stitch to create different effects.

Fabric
- 66 x 40cm (26 x 16 inches) white cotton
- 66 x 40cm (26 x 16 inches) cotton voile backing fabric

Thread
DMC six-stranded cotton thread:
- 964 Light sea green
- 168 Very light pewter
- B5200 Snow white
- 744 Pale yellow
- 745 Light pale yellow
- 169 Light pewter
- 351 Coral
- 350 Medium coral

Needles
- Embroidery: size 7, 9

Other
- Foam board
- Matching sewing thread
- Frame

transfer
- Centre the birdhouse design on the white cotton fabric and transfer using one of the methods given on page 17. Overlock or tack the cotton voile to the back of the fabric.

embroider
- Embroider the design according to the instructions.
- When the embroidery is complete, place it face down on a towel and iron it from the back.

mount
- Cut a 56 x 30cm (22 x 12 inch) rectangle of foam board.
- Centre the embroidered fabric on top of the board and pin it in place by sticking pins through the fabric and into the sides of the board. Smooth the fabric over the edges of the board as you pin.
- Turn it over and fold opposite sides of the fabric over the board. Use a long piece of sewing thread and make small stitches in first the top then bottom fabric to create a zigzag pattern – you're lacing the fabric to hold it in place. Pull the thread taut before securing the end, taking care not to bend the board. Do the same with the remaining sides.
- Frame the work as desired.

Embroidery instructions and design Enlarge by 250%

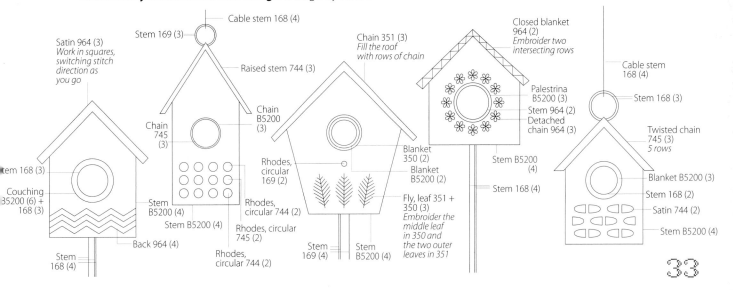

Stacked bowls tea towel

DISHES FOR DOING THE DISHES

A row of stem stitch worked in a single strand of thread outlines the leaves on the bottom bowl without overwhelming the fly stitch leaf detail inside. And alternating the colours of the rows of chain stitch on the bowl in the middle gives the illusion of striped crockery. If you want to match your threads to your tea towel, match light for light and dark for dark colours to get the same effect.

Needleturn appliqué is a good way to attach embroidery to a ready-made household item such as a tea towel, with the added advantage that the back of the embroidery is hidden automatically. It's also a clever way to add a touch of embroidery to patterned fabric that would otherwise overwhelm the hand stitching.

Fabric
- 25 x 25cm (10 x 10 inches) white cotton
- 25 x 25cm (10 x 10 inches) white cotton voile backing fabric

Thread
DMC six-stranded cotton thread:
- 347 Very dark salmon
- B5200 Snow white
- 164 Light forest green
- 168 Very light pewter
- 169 Light pewter
- 598 Light turquoise

Needles
- Embroidery: size 7, 9

Other
- Tea towel
- Cardstock, for template
- Matching sewing thread

Tea towels are quick and easy to make if you can't find a ready-made one that appeals to you. Simply cut a rectangle of suitable cotton fabric and hem the edges.

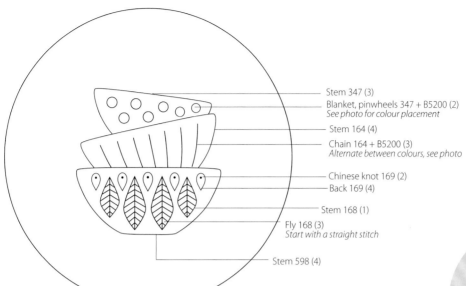

Stem 347 (3)
Blanket, pinwheels 347 + B5200 (2)
See photo for colour placement
Stem 164 (4)
Chain 164 + B5200 (3)
Alternate between colours, see photo
Chinese knot 169 (2)
Back 169 (4)
Stem 168 (1)
Fly 168 (3)
Start with a straight stitch
Stem 598 (4)

SKILL
LEVEL

Machine stitch the appliqué circle to the tea towel as an alternative to hand appliqué, using contrasting thread for added detail.

prepare

- Draw a circle on the cardstock measuring 13.5cm (5¼ inches) in diameter and cut it out neatly. You'll use this to create a round, needleturn appliqué circle.

transfer

- Transfer the bowls design onto the white cotton using one of the methods given on page 17. Include the circle cutting line. Overlock or tack the voile to the back of the fabric.

embroider

- Embroider the design according to the instructions.
- Iron the fabric face down on a towel when the embroidery is done, before cutting it out.

cut

- Check that the traced-on cutting line hasn't distorted during stitching and redraw it if necessary before cutting out the appliqué circle.

sew

- Stitch a row of small tacking stitches close to the edge of the fabric circle by hand. Leave tails of thread at either end.
- Position the card template in the centre of the embroidered circle, with the embroidery facing down, and pull the ends of the tacking thread to gather the fabric around the card circle. Pull the threads as taut as possible without snapping them and tie in a knot.
- Make sure the fabric is lying smoothly around the card before ironing firmly around the edge to create a hem that will stay in place when the card is removed.
- Remove the tacking and card, and pin the appliqué circle to the bottom, right-hand corner of the tea towel.
- Stitch in place by hand with small invisible stitches, as you would for needleturn appliqué.

Tulips

BLUE BLOOMS FOR AN ILLUSTRATIVE LOOK

The flowers are embroidered using simple stitches that won't alter the shape of the petals and which keep the outlines smooth. Lines and a sickle shape add weight to the floral aspect of the design – balancing the petals with the stems and leaves – and brings in additional colour.

Thread

DMC six-stranded cotton thread:

- 964 Light sea green
- 168 Very light pewter
- 907 Light parrot green

Needles

- Embroidery: size 7, 9

SKILL LEVEL

A double row of stitching adds weight to the stem of the flower without affecting the smoothness of the line.

Enlarge by 150%

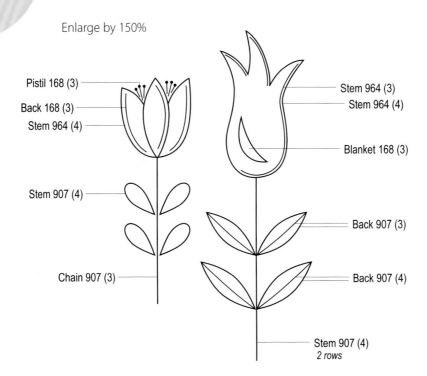

Pistil 168 (3)
Back 168 (3)
Stem 964 (4)
Stem 907 (4)
Chain 907 (3)

Stem 964 (3)
Stem 964 (4)
Blanket 168 (3)
Back 907 (3)
Back 907 (4)
Stem 907 (4)
2 rows

SKILL LEVEL ✗✗✗

SKILL LEVEL ✗✗✗

Pine trees

Salt and pepper

Double seeding and sheaf filling stitches denote pine needles in this design. Try to keep your straight stitches in line and evenly spaced to get the best effect – use the weave of the fabric as a guide where you can.

Long and short stitch is usually employed to shade areas of embroidery with dark to light colour, but here it's used to create the effect of snow on distant mountaintops.

Thread

DMC six-stranded cotton thread:

Thread

DMC six-stranded cotton thread:

Needles

• Embroidery: size 7, 9

• 798 Dark Delft blue
• B5200 Snow white
• 169 Light pewter grey
• 347 Very dark salmon

Needles

• Embroidery: size 7, 9

• 502 Blue green
• 169 Light pewter grey

Enlarge by 250%

Enlarge by 200%

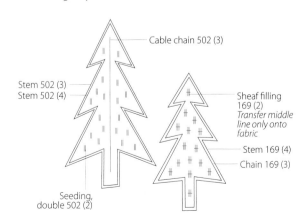

Cable chain 502 (3)

Stem 502 (3)
Stem 502 (4)

Sheaf filling
169 (2)
*Transfer middle
line only onto
fabric*

Stem 169 (4)

Chain 169 (3)

Seeding,
double 502 (2)

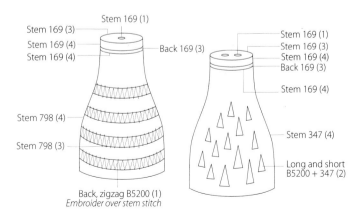

Stem 169 (1)

Stem 169 (3)
Stem 169 (4)
Stem 169 (4)

Back 169 (3)

Stem 169 (1)
Stem 169 (3)
Stem 169 (4)
Back 169 (3)

Stem 169 (4)

Stem 798 (4)

Stem 798 (3)

Stem 347 (4)

Long and short
B5200 + 347 (2)

Back, zigzag B5200 (1)
Embroider over stem stitch

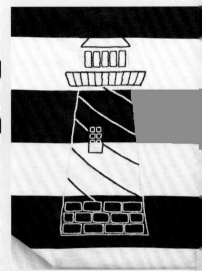

coastal

*Casually elegant with a nautical feel,
in crisp and calming hues*

Fabric
- 0.5m (20 inches) white linen
- 0.5m (20 inches) white cotton voile backing fabric

Thread
DMC six-stranded cotton thread:
- 321 Red
- Blanc White

Needles
- Embroidery: size 7
- Milliner: size 5

Other
- 2m (6½ feet) navy-and-white-striped piping
- 35cm (14 inch) zip, white
- 45 x 45cm (18 x 18 inch) cushion inner
- Matching sewing thread

Piping the edges of a cushion always adds an elegant touch.

Coral cushion

A SPLASH OF COLOUR FROM THE OCEAN

The coral design on the cushion is simple and elegant, with texture introduced through the use of knotted embroidery stitches. There's some freestyle stitching involved, as the design is outlined first and then filled in with more textural stitches. It takes a fair amount of thread, so have a few extra skeins on hand.

The navy-and-white-striped piping around the edges of the cushion reinforces the nautical nature of the design. The colours complement the bold red thread and the piping enhances the embroidery further by 'framing' the design.

prepare

- Cut a 50 x 50cm (20 x 20 inch) piece of white cotton and a 50 x 50cm (20 x 20 inch) piece of cotton voile. Draw a 43 x 43cm (17 x 17 inch) square on the fabric.

transfer

- Centre the coral embroidery design on the white cotton and transfer using one of the methods on page 17. Overlock or tack the voile to the back of the fabric.

embroider

- Other than the final French knots, the entire design is embroidered in 321.

- Embroider the design according to the instructions. First outline the coral in stem stitch, then embroider a second row inside the first.

- Next stitch long rows of Palestrina and coral stitch down the centre of the coral branches to create texture. Fill in the remaining space with stem stitch, using four strands of thread.

- Finally, embroider French knots in four strands of Blanc where indicated on the pattern, on top of the rows of red embroidery, if necessary.

- Press the finished work by placing it face down on a towel and ironing it from the back.

cut

- Check that the cutting lines haven't distorted during stitching and redraw them if necessary, then cut out the embroidered cushion front.

- Cut two rectangular panels for the cushion back: 43 x 38cm (17 x 15 inches) and 43 x 15cm (17 x 6 inches).

sew

- Sew the piping to the right side of the embroidered cushion front, 1.2cm (½ inch) from the edge using the zipper foot of your sewing machine to stitch as close to the piping as possible. The raw edges of the piping and your cushion front should be on the same side. Start in the centre of the bottom edge of the cushion, round off the corners and cross the two ends of piping over each other neatly when you get back to the start point, in such a way that the loose ends will be stitched into the seam when you attach the back of the cushion.

- Overlock or zigzag the zip edges of each panel, then iron a 1.2cm (½ inch) hem into the smaller back panel and a 5cm (2 inch) hem into the larger panel. Using a suitable fabric marker, draw a line across the width of the larger piece of fabric, 4.5cm (1¾ inches) above the fold.

- Insert the zip: place the zip face down and centred on the top edge of the smaller piece of fabric. Tack it in place, keeping the zip's teeth just below the ironed fold line. Stitch by machine along the fold line, using the zipper foot of your sewing machine. Fold the ironed hem back into place so that the zip flips over and is facing upwards/right side up. Position the larger (upper) piece of the cushion back so that the 5cm (2 inch) fold overlaps the lower piece by 4cm (1½ inches). (Lay the two pieces on top of the cushion front at this stage to check for size and adjust the overlap if necessary.) Tack the upper edge of the zip to the top of the cushion back and topstitch across the width of the cushion back – along the drawn-on line – using the zipper foot. Remove the line with a damp cloth or as advised by the fabric marker manufacturer.

- Open the zip halfway and pin the embroidered front to the cushion back, right sides facing.

- Using the stitching line from the piping as a guide, stitch over it, sewing around all four sides and joining the front and back of the cushion. Check that the piping is caught neatly between the front and back of the cushion, then overlock or zigzag the raw edges to finish off the seams.

- Turn the cushion cover the right way round through the zip opening and press with an iron from the back if necessary.

Embroider knotted stitches first when filling in a shape – you need the needle room.

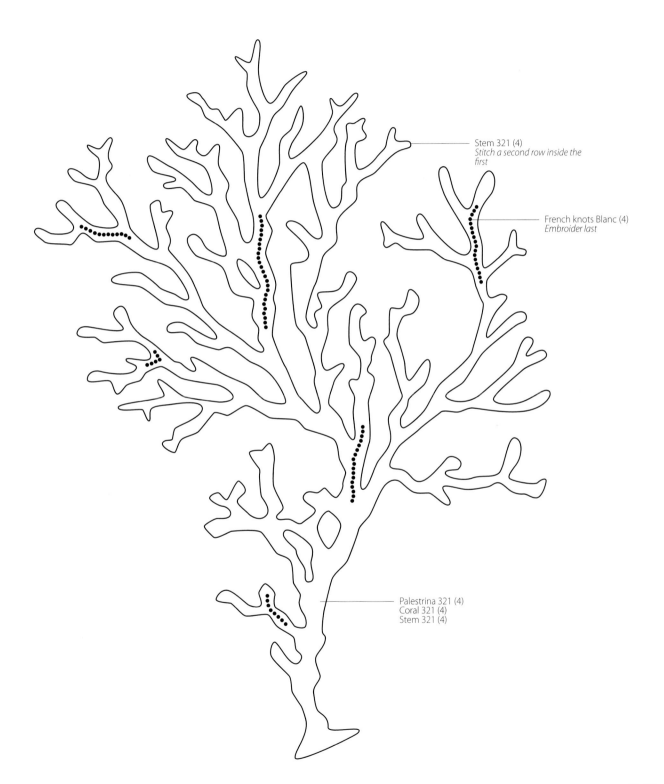

Stem 321 (4)
Stitch a second row inside the first

French knots Blanc (4)
Embroider last

Palestrina 321 (4)
Coral 321 (4)
Stem 321 (4)

Hanging fish

MIX AND MATCH A SHOAL

Blanket stitch is extremely versatile with lots of variations, but closed blanket stitch seems to better resemble scales, as do rows of isolated fly stitches. The latter are irregular with a hand-drawn look so you don't have to fuss too much over uniformity of stitching.

One fish has a navy-and-white-striped backing, the other a sand-coloured linen – choose the one that best suits your home's décor. You could pick your backing fabric first and then your embroidery threads to match. Either way, these decorative hanging fish add a subtle seaside touch to any home.

Fabric
- 28 x 38cm (11 x 15 inches) white cotton
- 28 x 38cm (11 x 15 inches) white cotton voile backing fabric
- 23 x 13cm (9 x 5 inches) navy-and-white-striped cotton
- 23 x 13cm (9 x 5 inches) natural linen

Thread
DMC six-stranded cotton thread:
- 3325 Light baby blue
- 312 Very dark baby blue
- 3033 Very light mocha brown
- 165 Very light moss green
- 445 Light lemon yellow
- 964 Light sea green

Needles
- Embroidery: size 7

Other
- 1m (39 inches) cord
- Stuffing
- Matching sewing thread

Experiment with the length of the securing stitch when doing fly stitch to adapt it to your needs.

Templates, embroidery instructions and design

Enlarge by 200%

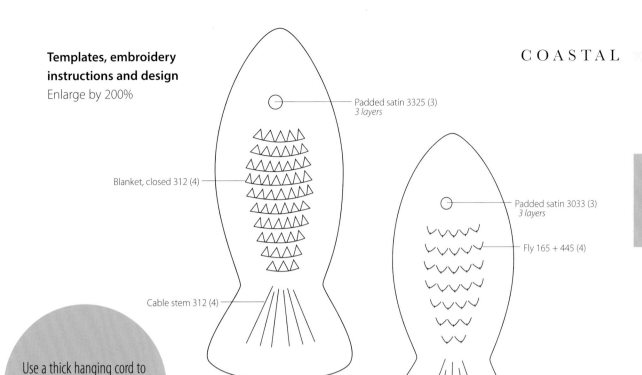

Padded satin 3325 (3)
3 layers

Blanket, closed 312 (4)

Cable stem 312 (4)

Padded satin 3033 (3)
3 layers

Fly 165 + 445 (4)

Back 964 (6)

Use a thick hanging cord to help create the 'mouth' of the fish and add weight.

transfer

- Transfer the fish designs onto the white cotton using one of the methods given on page 17. Include the cutting lines. Overlock or tack the voile to the back of the fabric.

embroider

- Embroider the designs according to the instructions.
- Iron the back of the embroidery, placed face down on a towel, when complete.

cut

- Cut out the fish along the traced-on cutting lines.
- Cut out two more fish shapes, one from each of the backing fabrics.
- Cut two lengths of cord, one 33cm (13 inches) and the other 38cm (15 inches).

sew

- Fold the pieces of cord in half to create loops, and pin one to the front (right side) of each embroidered fish, at the head, with the cord hanging downwards over the body. Sew in place close enough to the edge of the fabric so that the stitching will fall inside the seam.
- Tack each embroidered fish to its backing fabric with right sides facing, then machine stitch around the edges using a 0.6cm (¼ inch) seam. Leave a gap down one side of the fish for turning.
- Remove the tacking, trim the cord, notch the fabric around the head and tail to eliminate bulk and clip the curves where the tail meets the body to allow it to splay, and then turn the fish the right way round through the gap.
- Stuff until nice and firm, but not bulging, and stitch closed by hand with small, invisible stitching.

Nautical knot napkins

AN ADDITIONAL TOUCH OF CLASS FOR ALREADY CLASSY LINEN NAPKINS

The rope-like look of stem stitch is ideal for this project. Take your time when tracing on the pattern as uniformity makes these designs. I've used four shades of navy blue for the four different knots, but you might want to keep them all the same colour.

Napkins are one of the easiest things to sew as you're really just hemming a square of fabric. You could simply square off the corners, but it's worth going to the extra effort of mitring them as this simple technique transforms napkins from weekday supper to fine dining.

Fabric
- 1.2m (4 feet) natural cotton-linen blend

Thread
DMC six-stranded cotton thread:
- 322 Dark baby blue
- 312 Very dark baby blue
- 803 Ultra very dark baby blue
- 336 Navy blue

Needles
- Embroidery: size 8

Other
- Matching sewing thread

Use half stem stitches at the points to reduce bulk.

SKILL
LEVEL

Embroidery instructions and design

Enlarge by 250%

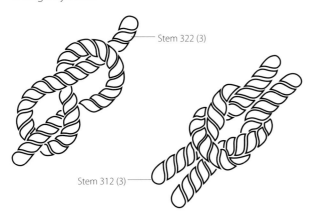

Stem 322 (3)

Stem 312 (3)

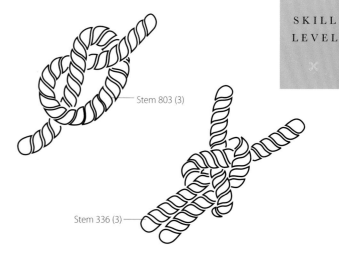

Stem 803 (3)

Stem 336 (3)

prepare

- Cut the fabric into four 56 x 56cm (22 x 22 inch) squares and draw a 50 x 50cm (20 x 20 inch) square on each.

transfer

- Transfer the knot designs onto the bottom right-hand corner of each drawn on square, leaving enough space to the right and below for the hem. Use one of the methods given on page 17 to transfer the designs.

embroider

- Embroider the designs according to the instructions.
- There is no backing fabric for this project, so either start with a small double stitch and embroider over it or use a waste knot. Knot the end of your thread and take it down through the fabric a few inches from your start point, then snip off the knot when you're done and weave the thread neatly through the back of the stitching to secure it. To end, take your thread through to the back of the fabric and weave it back along the row of stitching you've just finished.
- When done, place the embroidered sections of the fabric face down on a towel and iron from the back.

cut

- Check that the cutting lines haven't distorted during stitching and redraw them if necessary before cutting out each of the napkins.

sew

- Press and then machine stitch a 2.5cm (1 inch) doublefold hem around the edge of each napkin. Mitre the corners.

A broad hem adds to
the elegance of the
finished napkins.

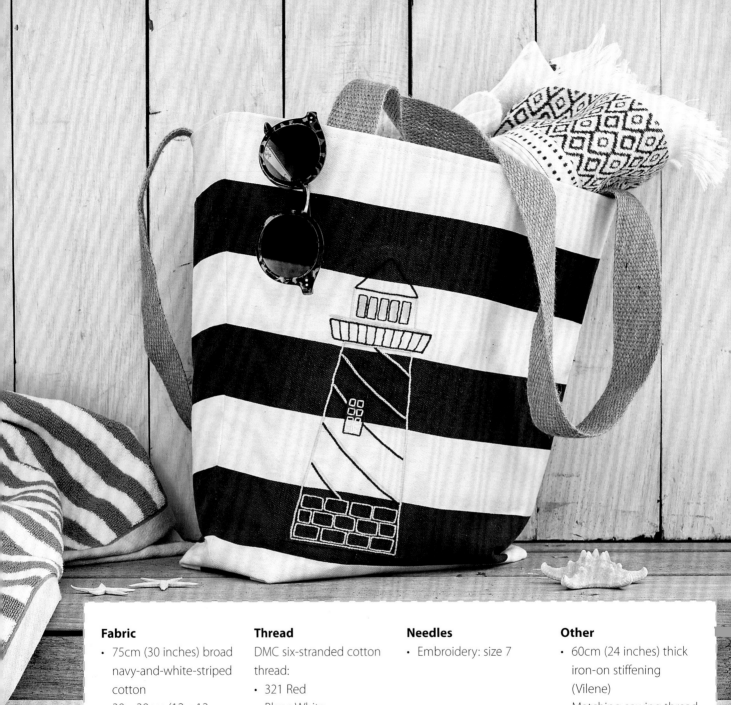

Fabric

- 75cm (30 inches) broad navy-and-white-striped cotton
- 30 x 30cm (12 x 12 inches) cotton voile backing fabric
- 75cm (30 inches) white cotton lining

Thread

DMC six-stranded cotton thread:
- 321 Red
- Blanc White
- 336 Navy blue
- 3033 Very light mocha brown

Needles

- Embroidery: size 7

Other

- 60cm (24 inches) thick iron-on stiffening (Vilene)
- Matching sewing thread
- 1m (39 inches) hessian webbing, 40mm (1½ inches) wide

Use webbing to add detail and eliminate having to sew bag straps from scratch.

Beach bag

A ROOMY BAG IN NAUTICAL STRIPES – PERFECT FOR A DAY AT THE BEACH

This is an easy design to embroider; the trickiest part is finding a good navy-and-white-striped fabric that isn't too thick to push a needle through easily.

The beach bag is a fairly simple one to make and the inner pocket is optional, or you could add additional pockets. The squared-off base and thick stiffening make it large and sturdy enough to hold towels, sunscreen, hats, sunglasses, a book, bucket, spade, bats, ball… whatever you need for a day in the sun.

transfer

- Transfer the lighthouse design and cutting lines for the front of the bag onto the navy-and-white-striped fabric using dressmakers' carbon as explained on page 17 – alternate between white and blue carbon so the design is visible on both colour stripes. Tack the square of cotton voile to the back of the fabric, behind the area to be embroidered.

embroider

- Embroider the design according to the instructions.
- When done, place the embroidery face down on a towel and iron from the back.

cut

- Check that the traced-on cutting lines haven't distorted during stitching and redraw them if necessary before cutting out the front of the bag.
- Use the bag front as a template to cut out the bag back from the navy-and-white-striped fabric (line up the stripes), two pieces of iron-on stiffening and two pieces of white lining.

- Optional: Cut a 25.5 x 15cm (10 x 6 inch) rectangle from the white lining for a patch pocket inside the bag.
- Cut two 80cm (31 inch) lengths of webbing for the straps.

sew

- Optional: Overlock or zigzag the edges of the patch pocket, then machine stitch a 1.2cm (½ inch) hem into one of the longer sides to form the top edge of the pocket. Press 1.2cm (½ inch) hems into the remaining three sides, position the pocket where desired on one of the pieces of lining fabric and topstitch it to the right side of the lining with a double row of stitching – one row close to the edge of the pocket and another close to the overlocked edge of the ironed hem. Swivel your fabric at the bottom corners with the machine needle in the down position.
- Remove the tacking holding the cotton voile in place, and fuse a piece of stiffening to the back of each of the two striped bag pieces. Lay the bag front face down on a towel when doing this.
- Pin each handle of the bag to the right side of a piece of navy-and-white-striped fabric with 2.5cm (1 inch) sticking out and the straps lying over the fabric. Position the handles about 10cm (4 inches)

Template and embroidery design

Enlarge by 500%

Use three long strands of thread doubled over – it's easier to pull six rather than 12 strands of thread through the fabric.

from either side of the bag, being careful not to twist the straps. Stitch in place close to the fabric edge, so the stitching falls inside the 1.2cm (1½ inch) seam once the lining has been attached.

• Pin the front and back of the bag each to a piece of lining fabric, right sides facing, and join along the top edges using a 1.2cm (½ inch) seam, securing the handles as you stitch. If adding the patch pocket, decide if you want it against the front or back of the bag (I've put it against the back of the bag) and attach it to the corresponding piece of lining fabric. Press the seams.

• Open the two pieces again so they're lying flat and pin the striped outer sides of the bag together and the linings together, right sides facing and so the centre seams line up. Line up the stripes on the outside of the bag. Stitch all the way around using a generous 1.2cm (½ inch) seam for the lining and a scant 1.2cm (½ inch) seam for the striped outside of the bag. Start on the bottom edge of the lining – leaving about an 18cm (7 inch) gap for turning – and work your way around, swivelling your fabric with the needle in the down position at the corners.

• Press the seams open.

• To create the squared-off base of the bag, line up the side seam at each corner with the bottom seam to form a triangle – keep the seams open. Measure 5cm (2 inches) from the top point, along the seams, and stitch across the bottom of the 'triangle' at this 5cm (2-inch) mark, perpendicular to the side and bottom seams. Do this for the outside of the bag as well as the lining.

• Turn the bag the right way round through the gap in the bottom of the lining.

• Pin the seams where the top edges of the bag and lining meet to keep them open, and keep the triangular flaps at the base of the bag in place (folded towards the base of the bag rather than up the sides) with a few securing stitches through the seam fabric before stitching the gap in the lining closed by hand with invisible stitching.

• Push the lining into the bag and press the seams gently.

• Topstitch around the top edge of the bag for added detail and a neat finish, and to reinforce the straps.

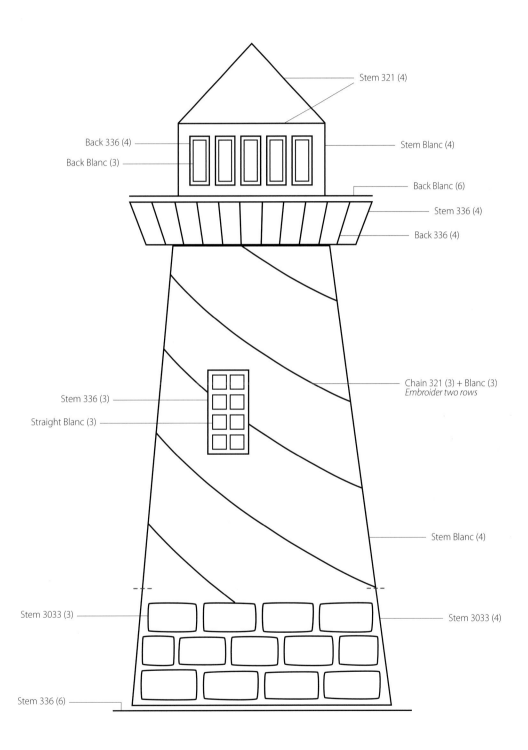

Stem 321 (4)

Back 336 (4)

Back Blanc (3)

Stem Blanc (4)

Back Blanc (6)

Stem 336 (4)

Back 336 (4)

Chain 321 (3) + Blanc (3)
Embroider two rows

Stem 336 (3)

Straight Blanc (3)

Stem Blanc (4)

Stem 3033 (3)

Stem 3033 (4)

Stem 336 (6)

Wave towel tags

Grading thread colours is an easy way to introduce variety into a simple embroidery design that uses only one stitch, as is differing the number of strands used for rows of stitching. You want a difference of two or three strands for the latter.

Towel tags are quick and easy to embroider; these wave tags add a splash of the sea to your hand towels, but they're also a good idea for bath towels. Vary the thread colours of the two designs to make each individual towel easy to identify – especially handy when you have guests staying over. Or add a touch of hand stitching if you're giving sumptuous bath sheets as a gift.

The embroidery designs can be enlarged for bigger towel tags without any adjustment to the embroidery instructions.

Fabric
- 30 x 30cm (12 x 12 inches) navy cotton
- 30 x 30cm (12 x 12 inches) cotton voile backing fabric
- 0.5m (20 inches) white cotton towelling OR two hand towels

Thread
DMC six-stranded cotton thread:
- 775 Very light baby blue
- 3841 Pale baby blue
- 3325 Light baby blue
- 3755 Baby blue
- 334 Medium baby blue
- 322 Dark baby blue
- 312 Very dark baby blue
- Blanc White

Needles
- Embroidery: size 7, 9

Other
- Matching sewing thread

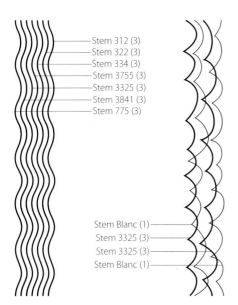

Stem 312 (3)
Stem 322 (3)
Stem 334 (3)
Stem 3755 (3)
Stem 3325 (3)
Stem 3841 (3)
Stem 775 (3)

Stem Blanc (1)
Stem 3325 (3)
Stem 3325 (3)
Stem Blanc (1)

SKILL
LEVEL

transfer

- Draw two rectangles onto the navy cotton fabric, measuring 17 x 7cm (6¾ x 2¾ inches). Centre a wave design in each rectangle and transfer using white dressmakers' carbon as explained on page 17. Overlock or tack the voile to the back.

embroider

- Embroider the designs according to the instructions.
- When the embroidery is done, place it face down on a towel and iron from the back.

cut

- If making the towels, cut two rectangles measuring 56 x 40cm (22 x 16 inches), or your chosen size. Add on 5cm (2 inches) for the hems.
- Check that the cutting lines haven't distorted during stitching and redraw them if necessary before cutting out each of the tags.

sew

- If making the towels, stitch a 1.2cm (½ inch) doublefold hem around the edge of each towel. Mitre the corners.

For sharp stem stitch points: Take your thread to the back at each point, loop it through the previous stitch to secure it and bring it back up through the same hole before continuing to stitch.

- Pin the long sides of each tag together, right sides facing, and machine stitch using a 0.6cm (¼ inch) hem to form a tube.
- Press the seam open (on a towel again to avoid squashing the embroidery) and turn the tube the right way round (attaching a safety pin to one end and threading it through the tube works well for this).
- Fold the short, raw edges in by 0.6cm (¼ inch) and iron in place.
- Fold the tag in half so the embroidery is on the outside and hand stitch the open ends together with invisible stitching.
- Stitch a tag to the centre of each towel using your sewing machine. Match your sewing thread to your towel and your bobbin thread to your tag.

Anchor

The secret to good whipped chain stitch is to use one strand of thread less for the whipping as this creates stripes of an even width. Use contrasting thread colours to striking effect.

Thread

DMC six-stranded cotton thread:

- 312 Very dark baby blue
- 321 Red
- Blanc White

Needles

- Embroidery: size 7, 9

Enlarge by 200%

Stem 312 (2)
Whipped chain 321 (4) + Blanc (3)
Stem 312 (3)
Back 312 (4)
Straight 312 (2) Embroider over back stitch
Stem 312 (3)

Compass

The symmetry of this mariner's compass design is what makes it impactful, and maintaining the symmetry through colour enhances this impact.

Thread

DMC six-stranded cotton thread:

- 932 Light antique blue
- 472 Ultra light avocado green
- Blanc White
- 3033 Very light mocha brown
- 317 Pewter grey

Needles

- Embroidery: size 7, 9
- Milliner: size 7

Enlarge by 200%

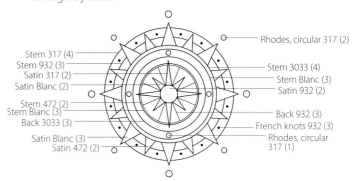

Stem 317 (4)
Stem 932 (3)
Satin 317 (2)
Satin Blanc (2)
Stem 472 (2)
Stem Blanc (3)
Back 3033 (3)
Satin Blanc (3)
Satin 472 (2)
Rhodes, circular 317 (2)
Stem 3033 (4)
Stem Blanc (3)
Satin 932 (2)
Back 932 (3)
French knots 932 (3)
Rhodes, circular 317 (1)

SKILL LEVEL ✕ ✕ ✕

Sailor's swallow

Fishbone stitch was made for the beaks of birds – there's no other stitch that renders them quite as well.

SKILL LEVEL ✕ ✕

Shells

Calming but fresh colours make this trio of shells the perfect reminder of a seaside holiday.

Thread

DMC six-stranded cotton thread:
- 803 Ultra very dark baby blue
- 321 Red
- 964 Light sea green
- 445 Light lemon yellow

Needles
- Embroidery: size 7, 9

Thread

DMC six-stranded cotton thread:
- Blanc White
- 317 Pewter grey
- 932 Light antique blue
- 3033 Very light mocha brown
- 964 Light sea green
- 472 Ultra light avocado green
- 165 Very light moss green
- 445 Light lemon yellow

Needles
- Embroidery: size 7, 9
- Milliner: size 7,8

Enlarge by 200%

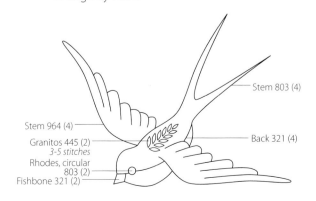

Stem 803 (4)

Stem 964 (4)

Granitos 445 (2)
3-5 stitches

Rhodes, circular
803 (2)

Fishbone 321 (2)

Back 321 (4)

Enlarge by 300%

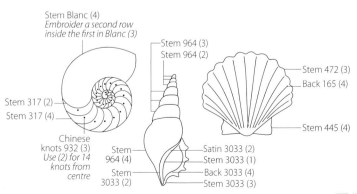

Stem Blanc (4)
Embroider a second row inside the first in Blanc (3)

Stem 964 (3)
Stem 964 (2)

Stem 317 (2)
Stem 317 (4)

Chinese
knots 932 (3)
Use (2) for 14 knots from centre

Stem
964 (4)

Stem
3033 (2)

Stem 472 (3)

Back 165 (4)

Stem 445 (4)

Satin 3033 (2)
Stem 3033 (1)
Back 3033 (4)
Stem 3033 (3)

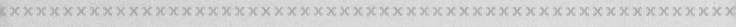

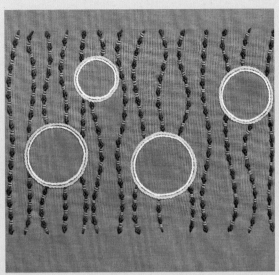

contemporary

*Minimalist designs with clean lines
and bold blocks of colour*

Fabric

- 0.5m (20 inches) grey cotton
- 0.5m (20 inches) cotton voile backing fabric
- 0.5m (20 inches) patterned cotton, for the lining

Thread

DMC six-stranded cotton thread:

- 517 Dark Wedgewood blue

Needles

- Embroidery: size 7

Other

- 2m (6½ feet) webbing, 40mm (1½ inches) wide, white
- White, grey sewing thread (match to fabric)

Bird silhouette tote

A SIMPLE, CLASSIC DESIGN FOR A STURDY TOTE BAG

The use of just one stitch – stem stitch – to embroider this design gives you room to focus on the simple pleasure of pulling a needle and thread through fabric in a rhythmic manner. It's a fairly quick design to embroider but uses at least two skeins of thread, so make sure you have enough to finish the embroidery before getting started.

The tote bag is a good size, with sturdy handles and a squared-off base, making it roomy enough to use for groceries, books, needlework supplies or even as an overnight bag. The bright, patterned lining adds a surprise detail in contrast to the simplicity of the bag's exterior.

transfer

- Draw a 102 x 48cm (40 x 18¾ inch) rectangle on the grey fabric – these are your cutting lines. Mark the fabric on each of the longer sides at 18cm (7 inches) and 41cm (16 inches). Position the embroidery design between these two marks, about 5cm (2 inches) in from the side of the rectangle, and transfer it to the fabric using one of the methods given on page 17. Overlock or tack the cotton voile to the back.

embroider

- Embroider the design according to the instructions.
- When you've finished embroidering, iron the fabric face down on a towel. Iron the rest of the fabric well before cutting out the rectangle.

cut

- Check that the cutting lines haven't distorted during stitching and redraw them if necessary before cutting out the tote.
- Cut the bag lining from the patterned fabric: 95 x 48cm (37½ x 18¾ inches).
- Cut two 86cm (34 inch) lengths of webbing for the straps.

Create your own design by tracing the outline of your desired shape and filling it with evenly spaced lines.

sew

- Iron a 0.6cm (¼ inch) hem into the top of each short end of the embroidered panel. Then make another 2.5cm (1 inch) fold and iron in place.

- Stitch the side seams together, hems unfolded, using a scant 1cm (³/₈ inch) seam. Press both side seams so they lie against either the back or the front of the bag and iron a fold into the bottom seam of the bag.

- With the bag inside out, line up the side seam with the bottom fold to form a triangle. Measure 5cm (2 inches) from the top point, along the side seam/bottom fold, and stitch across the bottom of the 'triangle' at the 5cm (2 inch) mark, perpendicular to the side seam and bottom fold. This creates the squared-off base of the bag.

- For the lining, stitch the side seams using a generous 1cm (³/₈ inch) seam and press both to either the front or the back of the bag lining. Stitch the bottom corners in the same way as the bag.

- Slide the lining into the tote, seams facing and bottom corners lining up. Make sure the bottom corner flaps are folded towards the base of the bag and your bag and lining seams lie in opposite directions to avoid bulk (if not, rotate the lining 180 degrees inside the bag).

- Match up the seams of the lining and the tote and pin in place along the top edge. The lining should reach the lower ironed hem fold of the tote, 3.25cm (1¼ inch) from the top.

- Fold the pressed hem down again, over the lining, and pin in place.

- Stitch a double row around the top edge of the bag to attach the lining to the tote.

- Overlock or zigzag stitch the ends of the straps to stop them fraying.

- Make a 7.5cm (3 inch) fold in each end of the webbing straps. Pin one strap to the front of the bag and the other to the back, 9cm (3½ inches) from the side seams and so the raw edges of the webbing are about 0.6mm (¼ inch) below the lip of the bag.

- Sew the handle ends to the bag using white sewing thread, but keep your bobbin grey. Stitch a rectangle and then an elongated cross inside it for strength and added detail.

Find other ways to add detail and contrast to a project when the embroidery is all one colour on solid fabric, such as using broad white webbing for the handles.

Stem 517 (4)

Midnight wall art

A STRIKING AND ORIGINAL DESIGN FOR A MODERN HOME

The moon is filled with isolated embroidery stitches arranged to form a repeat pattern, and then various patterns combined to create the whole. The tricky part is keeping your stitches as even as possible so you end up with a consistent pattern.

If you opt for a ready-made frame, look for one big enough to allow a bit of space around the embroidered design. Otherwise get your finished embroidery framed professionally, when it can be made to size. Ask your framer to use non-reflective glass so your work is more visible through it.

Fabric
50 x 50cm (20 x 20 inches)
white cotton
50 x 50cm (20 x 20 inches)
cotton voile backing fabric

Thread
DMC six-stranded cotton thread:
- 3799 Very dark pewter grey
- 726 Light topaz
- 727 Very light topaz
- 3078 Very light golden yellow

Needles
Embroidery: size 7, 9
Milliner: size 8

Other
- Foam board
- Sewing thread
- Frame

Imagine working inside a square when doing double cross stitch; it'll help to keep the stitches even.

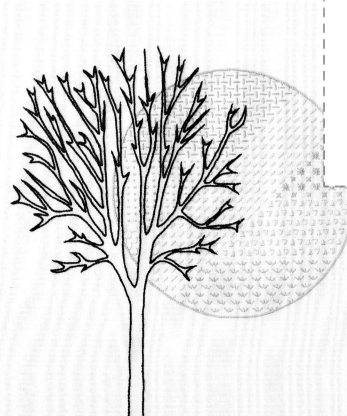

Enlarge by 250%

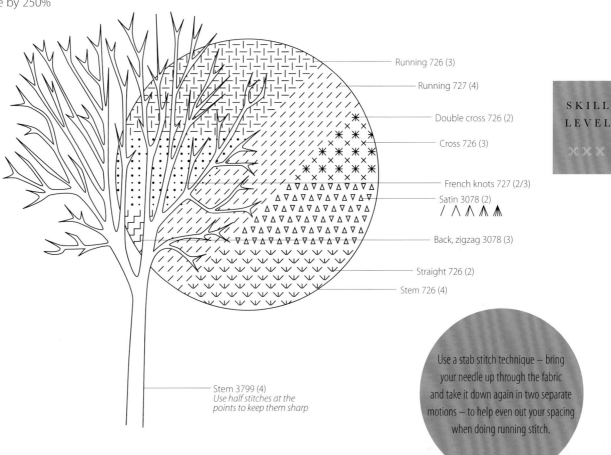

Running 726 (3)

Running 727 (4)

Double cross 726 (2)

Cross 726 (3)

French knots 727 (2/3)

Satin 3078 (2)

Back, zigzag 3078 (3)

Straight 726 (2)

Stem 726 (4)

SKILL
LEVEL

Stem 3799 (4)
*Use half stitches at the
points to keep them sharp*

Use a stab stitch technique – bring
your needle up through the fabric
and take it down again in two separate
motions – to help even out your spacing
when doing running stitch.

transfer

- Centre the design on the white cotton fabric and transfer using one of the methods given on page 17. Overlock or tack the cotton voile to the back of the fabric.

embroider

- Embroider the design according to the instructions. Use half stitches at the points of the branches to keep them nice and sharp: omit the last half-length stitch at the end of each row and, at the beginning of a row, bring your needle back up for your second stitch half a stitch length away from the start point. At each point, take your thread to the back and loop it under a stitch to secure it before coming up again through the same hole and continuing down the other side of the branch.

- For the moon, outline it first and then refer to the diagram to fill with embroidery.

- When complete, iron the embroidery face down on a towel.

mount

- Cut out a 43 x 43cm (17 x 17 inch) square of foam board.

- Centre the embroidered fabric on top of the board and pin it in place by sticking pins through the fabric and into the sides of the board. Smooth the fabric over the edges of the board as you pin.

- Turn it over and fold the opposite sides of the fabric over the board. Use a long piece of sewing thread and make small stitches in first the top then bottom fabric to create a zigzag pattern – you're lacing the fabric to hold it in place. Pull the thread taut before securing the end, taking care not to bend the board. Do the same with the remaining sides.

- Frame the embroidery as desired.

Use bold thread colours on dark fabric to ensure the embroidery shows up well.

Geometric laptop case

GEOMETRY ON THE OUTSIDE, BINARY ON THE INSIDE

The geometric shapes that make up the laptop cover design are easy to embroider as they're done in just three basic stitches. The repetition of solid and dashed lines is what holds the design together, as well as the grouping of strong, primary colours.

The measurements given are for a 33cm (13-inch) laptop. Measure your device first and adjust the measurements to fit it if necessary before you cut any fabric. Take care with the zippered insert and tack it in place first to make sewing it easier.

Fabric
- 80cm (32 inches) charcoal grey cotton
- 40 x 40cm (16 x 16 inches) cotton voile backing fabric

Thread
DMC six-stranded cotton thread:
- 817 Very dark coral red
- 349 Dark coral

- 727 Very light topaz
- 726 Light topaz
- 3078 Very light golden yellow
- 905 Dark parrot green
- 904 Very dark parrot green
- 906 Medium parrot green
- 907 Light parrot green
- 517 Dark

Wedgewood blue
- 3842 Very dark Wedgewood blue

Needles
- Embroidery: size 7

Other
- 40cm (16 inches) quilters' batting/ wadding
- Matching sewing thread

- 55cm (21 inch) zip
- 2.5m (8¼ feet) black bias binding, 20mm (¾ inch) wide (match to fabric)

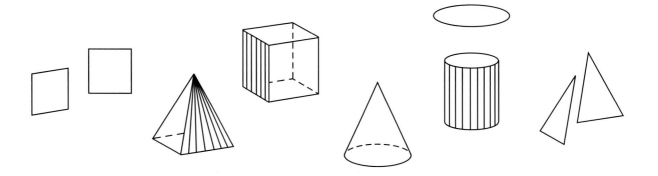

prepare

- Cut a 40 x 40cm (16 x 16 inch) square of grey fabric and draw a 37.5 x 28cm (14¾ x 11 inch) rectangle on it.

transfer

- Centre the embroidery design within the drawn-on rectangle and transfer it to the fabric using white dressmakers' carbon, as explained on page 17. Overlock or tack the cotton voile to the back of the fabric.

embroider

- Embroider the design according to the instructions.
- When the embroidery is complete, place the fabric face down on a towel and iron it from the back.

cut

- Check that the drawn-on cutting lines haven't distorted during stitching and redraw them if necessary before cutting out the embroidered panel of the laptop case.
- Cut three 37.5 x 28cm (14¾ x 11 inch) rectangles from the grey fabric.
- Cut two 37.5 x 28cm (14¾ x 11 inch) rectangles of batting.
- Cut two 70 x 4cm (26½ x 1½ inch) strips of grey fabric on the cross.

sew

- Sandwich the end of the zip between the ends of the two strips of grey fabric and stitch together using using a 1.2cm (½ inch) seam. Do the same at the other end of the zip and then flip the fabric back so that the zip emerges from between the two strips and you have a band of zip and fabric.
- Sandwich a piece of batting between the embroidered panel and another rectangle of grey fabric, and do the same for the back of the case using the remaining two pieces of grey fabric.
- Centre the zip along the top of the case (line up the halfway point of the zip with the halfway point of the top edge of the embroidered panel and pin then tack from there; the zip will lie 0.6cm (¼ inch) in from the edge and the fabric will line up with the edges of the front and back), then stitch the front of the case to the fabric section of the zip band, using a 1.2cm (½ inch) seam and with right sides together so the seam is showing on the right side. Round off the corners as you go. Open the zip a bit and then do the same with the back of the case.
- Bind the seams by hand with bias binding to neaten the inside of the case.
- Open the zip fully and turn the case the right way round through the opening.

Embroider the inner lines of the shapes first, then the outlines, for a neater finish.

Embroidery instructions

Full size

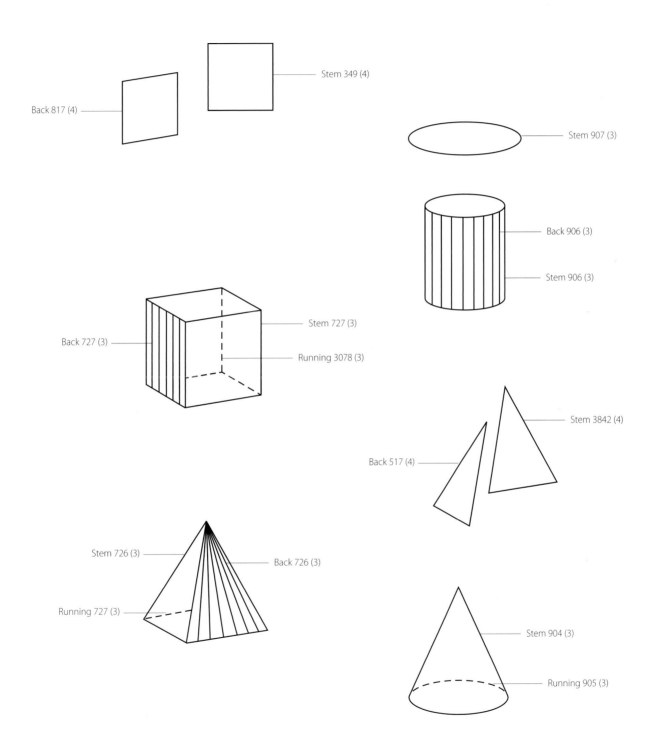

Back 817 (4)

Stem 349 (4)

Stem 907 (3)

Back 906 (3)

Stem 906 (3)

Stem 727 (3)

Back 727 (3)

Running 3078 (3)

Stem 3842 (4)

Back 517 (4)

Stem 726 (3)

Back 726 (3)

Running 727 (3)

Stem 904 (3)

Running 905 (3)

Fabric
- 30cm (12 inches) light grey cotton
- 30cm (12 inches) cotton voile backing fabric
- 30cm (12 inches) white cotton (for the lining)

Thread
DMC six-stranded cotton thread:
- 317 Pewter grey
- 318 Light steel grey
- 726 Light topaz
- B5200 Snow white

Needles
- Embroidery: size 7, 9

Other
- 30cm (12 inches) quilters' batting
- Matching sewing thread

Use the straight couching stitches to help the thread between Palestrina knots curve and follow the lines of the design.

Abstract tablet sleeve

A PRACTICAL, PADDED SLEEVE WITH CREATIVE STITCHING

Create texture by combining embroidery stitches. Couch down knotted stitches with straight stitches or straight stitches with knots – the possibilities are only as limited as your imagination.

The sleeve is open at one end, making it easy to slide your tablet in and out, but the fit is snug to stop it slipping out. The measurements given here are for an iPad Air 2. For any other iPad or tablet, measure your device first and add 1.2cm (½ inch) to the length and the width to create a little room in the sleeve. Then double the length and add 3.5cm (1¼ inches) for the seam and fold allowances. Add 4cm (1½ inches) to the width for the side seams and use these measurements when preparing your fabric. Position the embroidery design in the top half of the drawn-on rectangle.

prepare

- Cut a 66 x 28cm (26 x 11 inch) rectangle of grey fabric and draw a 54 x 22cm (21¼ x 8½ inch) rectangle on it. Make two positioning marks along each of the longer sides, 5cm (2 inches) and 23cm (9 inches) from a short end.

transfer

- Centre the embroidery design between the two positioning marks and transfer it to the fabric using one of the methods given on page 17. Overlock or tack the cotton voile to the back of the fabric.

embroider

- Embroider the design according to the instructions.

- Iron the embroidery from the back, placing it face down on a towel. Iron the rest of the sleeve before assembling it.

cut

- Check that the drawn-on cutting lines haven't distorted during stitching and redraw them if necessary before cutting.
- Cut a 54 x 22cm (21¼ x 8½ inch) piece of white cotton for the lining.
- Cut a 51.5 x 19cm (20¼ x 7½ inch) rectangle of batting.

sew

- Iron a 1.2cm (½ inch) hem into the short edge below the embroidery and one of the short edges of the white lining fabric, then fold them open again.

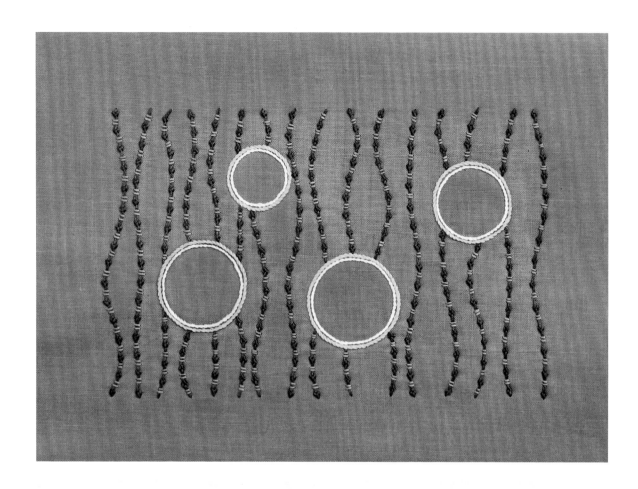

- Pin the embroidered panel to the white lining fabric, right sides and ironed hems facing, and stitch around three edges using a 1.2cm (½ inch) seam. Leave the short end with the ironed hems open.

- Turn the sleeve the right way round and push the corners out neatly.

- Slide the batting between the two layers so it lies snugly against the edges of the sleeve.

- Fold the ironed hems back down, one of them over the batting, and stitch closed by hand.

- Fold the sleeve in half and machine stitch the sides together, 0.6cm (¼ inch) from the edge.

The lining will show as a thin line down the edges of the sleeve, which adds a nice detail, so keep that in mind when choosing your lining fabric.

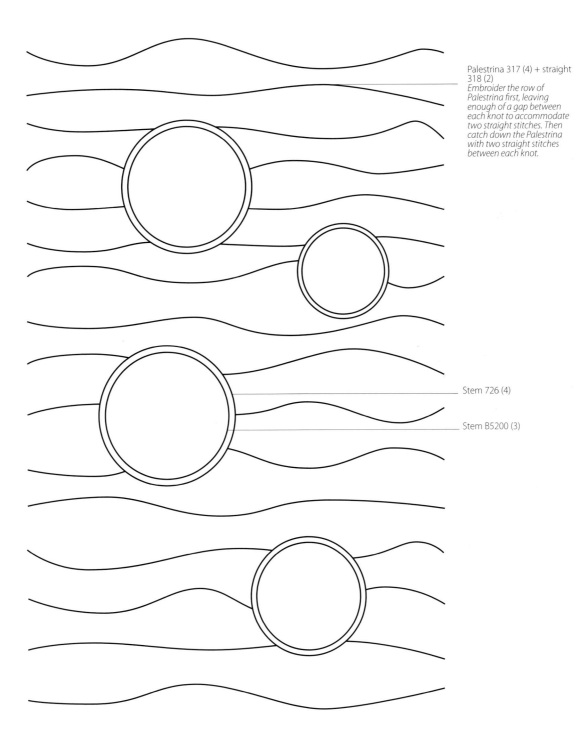

Palestrina 317 (4) + straight
318 (2)
*Embroider the row of
Palestrina first, leaving
enough of a gap between
each knot to accommodate
two straight stitches. Then
catch down the Palestrina
with two straight stitches
between each knot.*

Stem 726 (4)

Stem B5200 (3)

Fabric
- 61 x 26cm (24 x 10 inches) charcoal grey cotton
- 61 x 26cm (24 x 10 inches) cotton voile backing fabric

Thread
DMC six-stranded cotton thread:
- 318 Light steel grey
- 817 Very dark coral red
- B5200 Snow white

Needles
- Embroidery: size 7, 9

Other
- A5 notebook, 192 pages
- Sewing thread to match

When doing satin stitch, start in the centre and work outwards in first one direction then the other to fill the area.

Cassette tape notebook

GIVE A PLAIN NOTEBOOK A NATTY JACKET

Blanket stitch is perfect for the wheels of the cassette tape. I've kept the stitches fairly big and used three strands of thread to create a blocky look.

Measure your notebook first and adjust the pattern to fit if necessary. The cover should fit snugly to stop it from slipping off the notebook and to prevent the book sliding around inside it. The two pockets that slide over the covers of the notebook are handy for storing loose notes, business cards and sketches on serviettes.

prepare

- Draw a 58.5 x 23cm (23 x 9 inch) rectangle onto the charcoal fabric and place positioning marks along the top and bottom edges, 14cm (5½ inches) and 30cm (11¼ inches) from the right-hand edge.

transfer

- Centre the cassette tape design between the two positioning marks and transfer it using white dressmakers' carbon, as explained on page 17. Overlock or tack the cotton voile to the back.

embroider

- Embroider the design according to the instructions.
- Iron the embroidery face down on a towel. Iron the rest of the notebook cover before cutting it out.

cut

- Check that the drawn-on cutting lines haven't distorted during stitching and redraw them if necessary before cutting out the notebook cover.

sew

- Overlock or zigzag around all four edges of the embroidered panel.
- Stitch a 0.6cm (¼ inch) hem in each of the short sides of the notebook cover.
- With the right side of the fabric facing up, fold in the sides 13.5cm (5¼ inches) from the edge and stitch to the front and back of the notebook cover along the top and bottom edges, using a 0.6cm (¼ inch) seam.
- Turn the notebook cover the right way round and push out the corners neatly (the tips of a closed pair of sewing scissors work well for this). Iron the sides and seams flat, folding over the remaining sections of the top and bottom edges by 0.6cm (¼ inch) as you go, to form an unstitched hem that lines up with the seams.
- Bend the covers of the notebook back to slide them simultaneously into the front and back 'pockets' of the notebook cover.

Embroidery instructions and design
Full Size

Back B5200 (4)

Stem 318 (2)

Blanket 318 (3)

Stem 318 (2)

Satin 318 (2)

Rhodes, circular 318 (2)

Cross B5200 (2)

Stem B5200 (2)

Stem 817 (4)

Stem 817 (3)

Straight 817 (2)

Stem 318 (2)

Back, trellis B5200 (2)

Back B5200 (4)

Embroider the back stitch trellis
using a stab stitch technique to help
prevent the thread from splitting: bring
your needle up and take it down again
in two separate movements.

Beetle

Palestrina stitch is highly adaptable and it's used here with the knots spaced so as to create the interlocking pattern on the beetle's head. You could give this a different feel by using white thread on black fabric.

Thread

DMC six-stranded cotton thread:

- 310 Black

Needles

- Embroidery: size 7, 9
- Milliner: size 7

Start with a detached chain stitch and, instead of catching it down, continue with blanket for a neat start to a row of blanket stitch.

Full size

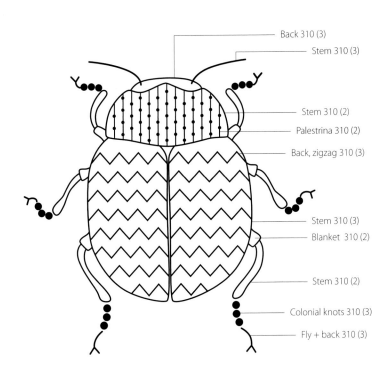

Back 310 (3)

Stem 310 (3)

Stem 310 (2)

Palestrina 310 (2)

Back, zigzag 310 (3)

Stem 310 (3)

Blanket 310 (2)

Stem 310 (2)

Colonial knots 310 (3)

Fly + back 310 (3)

Enlarge by 125%

Flower

Increasing the number of strands of thread from two for the smallest petals to four for the largest emphasises the subtle change in colour from the centre to the outer edges of the flower, bringing the design to life.

Thread
DMC six-stranded cotton thread:
- B5200 Snow white
- 3078 Very light golden yellow
- 727 Very light topaz
- 726 Light topaz

Needles
- Embroidery: size 7, 9

Take your time transferring designs that rely on symmetry and draw the lines as smoothly as possible

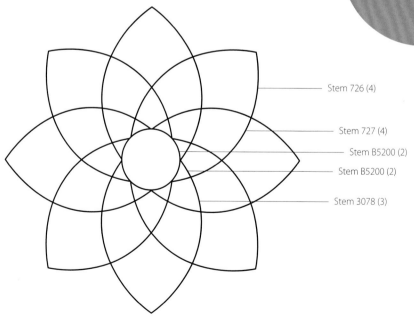

Stem 726 (4)

Stem 727 (4)

Stem B5200 (2)

Stem B5200 (2)

Stem 3078 (3)

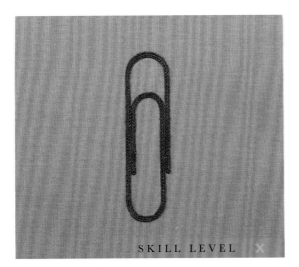

SKILL LEVEL x

Paperclip

This is a particularly simple design. Your initial row of stitching will determine the final shape of the paperclip, so take care when embroidering it.

Thread

DMC six-stranded cotton thread:

- 3842 Very dark Wedgewood blue

Needles

- Embroidery: size 7

Enlarge by 200%

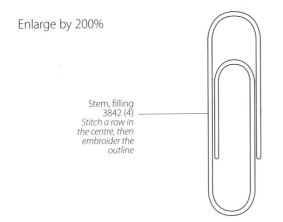

Stem, filling
3842 (4)
*Stitch a row in
the centre, then
embroider the
outline*

SKILL LEVEL x

Leaf

The veins of the leaf make up its shape as there is no outline, so take care when transferring the design to make sure you get your start and end points in the right places.

Thread

DMC six-stranded cotton thread:

- 905 Dark parrot green

Needles

- Embroidery: size 7

Enlarge by 200%

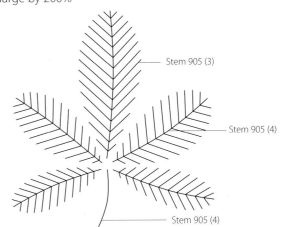

Stem 905 (3)

Stem 905 (4)

Stem 905 (4)

country

*A modern take on a much-loved,
cosy style*

Cat doorstop

WELCOME GUESTS WITH A CATFUL OF WILDFLOWERS STANDING SENTINEL AT THE DOOR

SKILL LEVEL

Every country home needs a cat and this project combines a beloved pet with fields of flowers. It employs a variety of colours and stitches to keep it interesting, from bright yellow cast-on petals to pink knotted buds that mingle with deep purple satin stitch foliage and vibrant green fishbone leaves.

A sandbag positioned in the bottom of the cat gives the doorstop weight while keeping it soft enough to avoid painful stubbed toes. The top is filled with toy stuffing, which gives the cat its shape.

Fabric
- 0.5m (20 inches) blue cotton
- 46 x 30cm (18 x 12 inches) cotton voile backing fabric
- 25cm (10 inches) white cotton

Thread
DMC six-stranded cotton thread:
- 3347 Medium yellow green
- 743 Medium yellow
- 987 Dark forest green
- 3779 Ultra very light rosewood
- 3328 Dark salmon
- 472 Ultra light avocado green
- 989 Forest green
- 3348 Light yellow green
- 3811 Very light turquoise
- 598 Light turquoise

- 744 Pale yellow
- 950 Light desert sand
- Blanc White
- 779 Dark cocoa
- 3860 Cocoa

Needles
- Embroidery: size 7, 9
- Milliner: size 8

Other
- Washed sand (used for kids' sandpits, available from hardware stores)
- Toy stuffing
- Sewing thread to match

BASE
CUT 1

SANDBAG SIDES
CUT 2

SANDBAG BASE
CUT 1

prepare

- Cut a 46 x 30cm (18 x 12 inch) piece of blue fabric.

transfer

- Transfer the embroidery design onto the blue cotton using one of the methods given on page 17, including the cutting lines. Overlock or tack the cotton voile to the back.

embroider

- Embroider the design according to the instructions.
- Place the fabric face down on a towel and iron the embroidery from the back when you've completed all the stitching.

cut

- Check that the traced-on cutting lines haven't distorted during stitching and redraw them if necessary, then cut out the embroidered front of the cat.
- Lay the front face down on the right side of the remaining blue fabric and use it as a template to cut out the back of the cat. You want a mirror image of the front.
- Use the template provided to cut out the base from the remaining blue fabric.
- Fold a section of the white cotton over on itself and use the template provided to cut out the sides of the sandbag – you want two pieces that mirror each other.
- Cut out the sandbag base using the template provided.

sew

- For the sandbag, join the two pieces of white fabric, right sides facing, at the sides using a 0.6cm (¼ inch) seam. Insert the sandbag base into the bottom and pin, tack, then stitch in place with a 0.6cm (¼ inch) seam. Turn the right way round and fill the bag with sand, then stitch the top closed by hand.
- Stitch the cat front to the back around the sides and head with right sides facing, using a 0.6cm (¼ inch) seam.
- Cut notches into the seam allowance on the convex curves (especially around the ears) and clip the concave curves (especially the neck). Then turn the cat the right way round and press the seams lightly.
- Sew a row of stitching around the bottom of the cat, 0.6cm (¼ inch) from the edge, and a similar row around the base as guides for when you come to attach the base.
- Fill the top of the cat with stuffing and then position the bag of sand so it sits solidly at the bottom of the cat, covered by the unstuffed fabric. Place some stuffing around the sides of the sandbag until the cat is stuffed firmly and is balancing nicely.
- Pin the base into the bottom of the cat – fold the seams over on the sewn lines as you go – and tack, then stitch in place by hand with a double strand of sewing thread, closing up the cat.

Template, embroidery instructions and design

Enlarge by 250%

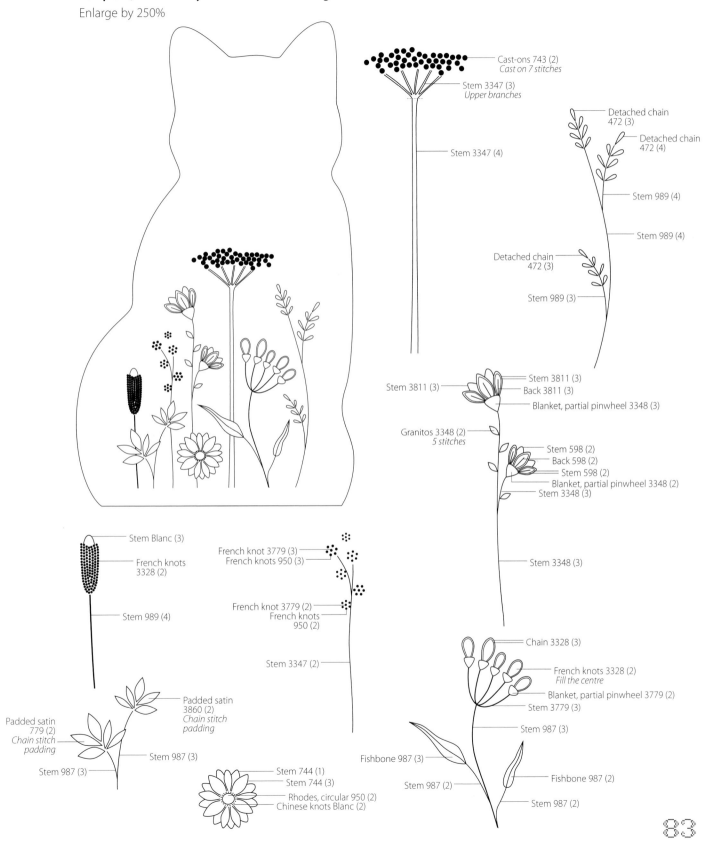

Cast-ons 743 (2)
Cast on 7 stitches

Stem 3347 (3)
Upper branches

Stem 3347 (4)

Detached chain 472 (3)

Detached chain 472 (4)

Stem 989 (4)

Stem 989 (4)

Detached chain 472 (3)

Stem 989 (3)

Stem 3811 (3)
Stem 3811 (3)
Back 3811 (3)
Blanket, partial pinwheel 3348 (3)

Granitos 3348 (2)
5 stitches

Stem 598 (2)
Back 598 (2)
Stem 598 (2)
Blanket, partial pinwheel 3348 (2)
Stem 3348 (3)

Stem 3348 (3)

Stem Blanc (3)

French knots 3328 (2)

French knot 3779 (3)
French knots 950 (3)

Stem 989 (4)

French knot 3779 (2)
French knots 950 (2)

Stem 3347 (2)

Chain 3328 (3)

French knots 3328 (2)
Fill the centre

Blanket, partial pinwheel 3779 (2)
Stem 3779 (3)

Stem 987 (3)

Padded satin 3860 (2)
Chain stitch padding

Padded satin 779 (2)
Chain stitch padding

Stem 987 (3)

Stem 987 (3)

Fishbone 987 (3)

Stem 987 (2)

Fishbone 987 (2)

Stem 987 (2)

Stem 744 (1)
Stem 744 (3)
Rhodes, circular 950 (2)
Chinese knots Blanc (2)

Leaf throw

A HAND-QUILTED THROW IN CRISP AUTUMNAL SHADES

Leaves, like flowers, are well suited to embroidery as you can use an abundance of stitches to embroider and embellish them.

The finished throw measures 142 x 142cm (56 x 56 inches), so look for fabric that's 150cm (59 inches) wide to avoid joins on the front of the throw. It's fine to buy 115cm-wide (45 inch) quilting fabric for the back, as you won't notice any joins once the throw has been quilted. You can also leave out the quilting altogether, omitting the batting, if you prefer a light throw for summer.

Fabric

- 1.5m (59 inches) white cotton/linen (minimum 150cm/59 inches wide)
- 1.5m (59 inches) white cotton voile backing fabric
- 1.5m (59 inches) 150cm (59 inches) wide OR 2.5m (98 inches) 115cm (45 inches) wide dusty red cotton
- 1m (40 inches) red-and-white-striped cotton fabric

Thread

DMC six-stranded cotton thread:
- 309 Dark rose
- 3328 Dark salmon
- 3779 Ultra very light rosewood
- 818 Baby pink
- Blanc White
- 963 Ultra very light dusty rose
- 3064 Desert sand
- 722 Light orange spice
- 744 Pale yellow
- 743 Medium yellow

Needles

- Embroidery: size 7

Other

- Bamboo quilters' batting
- White hand-quilting thread
- Matching sewing thread
- Soft lead pencil or water-soluble marker
- Quilting ruler
- Quilting pins (optional)

Quilters' batting is made from various materials and comes at different price points, from inexpensive polyester batting to pricier bamboo and cotton batting. If you can, invest in bamboo or cotton - the amount of time and effort spent hand embroidering an item justifies the added expense and it results in a better end product.

prepare

- Draw a 142 x 142cm (56 x 56 inch) square on the white fabric. Position it so the ends of the leaf stalks are 34cm (13½ inches) from the bottom line and the design is centred across the width; there should be about 16cm (6¼ inches) of space on either side of the design.

- Cut a 150 x 150cm (59 x 59 inch) square of cotton voile.

transfer

- Transfer the leaves onto the fabric using one of the methods given on page 17. Overlock or tack the square of cotton voile to the back.

embroider

- Embroider the design according to the instructions.

- Place the embroidered section of the throw face down on a towel and iron the back of the stitching. Iron the rest of the throw front, avoiding the embroidered section, before putting it together.

cut

- Check that the cutting lines haven't distorted during stitching and redraw them if necessary before cutting out the throw front.

- Cut and piece the dusty red cotton backing fabric if necessary to create a 150 x 150cm (59 x 59 inch) square.

- Cut a 150 x 150cm (59 x 59 inch) square of batting.

- Cut six 13cm (5-inch) wide strips from the striped fabric, perpendicular to the direction of the stripes. Cut two of these strips in half.

sew

- Draw quilting lines onto the embroidered front of the throw in a pattern of your choosing – I used a tartan-like design made up of straight lines grouped in twos vertically and threes horizontally to form checks. Avoid quilting over the embroidery and stop and start each line about 5cm (2 inches) in from the edge of the throw. A soft lead pencil or water-soluble marker works well for this, along with a quilting ruler.

- Sandwich the batting between the embroidered front and the backing fabric and either tack together with a few long rows of stitching or pin using quilters' safety pins. Smooth your fabric/batting out well as you add each layer.

- Quilt the throw using hand-quilting thread along the drawn-on lines.

- Check that the cutting lines haven't pulled during quilting and trim all three layers to size before attaching the flange.

- For the flange: Sew a half-length strip to each of the four full-length strips – use a 0.6cm (¼ inch) seam allowance and press the seams open. Draw two lines along the length of each strip, 1.2cm (½ inch) from the edge. Fold each strip in half lengthways and iron the fold in place, then open the fabric out again and press a 1.2cm (½ inch) hem into each edge using the drawn-on line as a guide. Draw a line 4cm (1½ inches) from the edge of the trimmed throw and attach the flange to the front of the throw as you would attach bias binding, using the line as a guide. Fold the flange over the raw edges of the throw and stitch to the back by hand. Mitre the corners. Tacking the flange in place first will make the hand stitching easier.

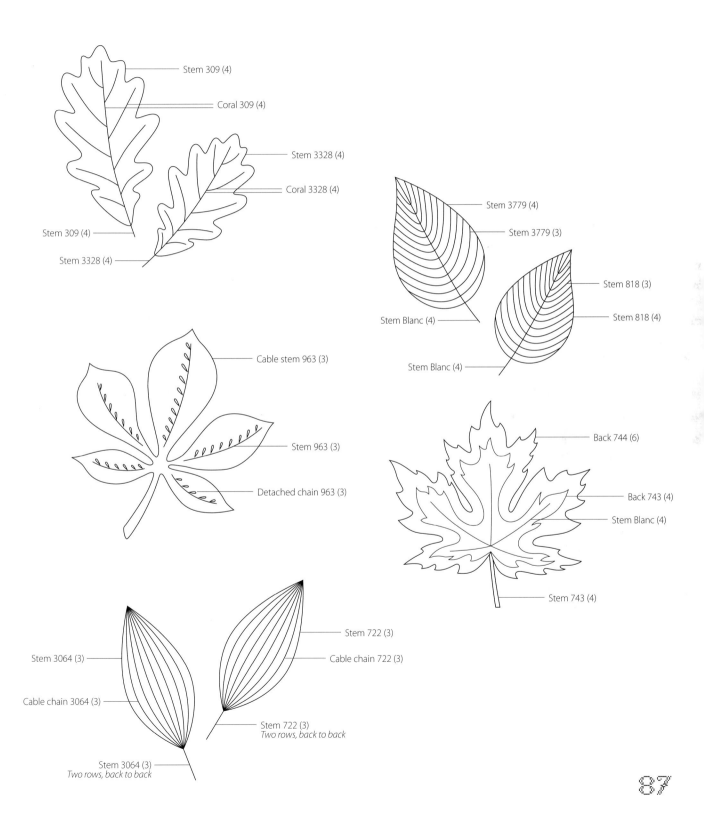

Stem 309 (4)

Coral 309 (4)

Stem 3328 (4)

Coral 3328 (4)

Stem 309 (4)

Stem 3328 (4)

Stem 3779 (4)

Stem 3779 (3)

Stem 818 (3)

Stem 818 (4)

Stem Blanc (4)

Stem Blanc (4)

Cable stem 963 (3)

Stem 963 (3)

Detached chain 963 (3)

Back 744 (6)

Back 743 (4)

Stem Blanc (4)

Stem 743 (4)

Stem 3064 (3)

Stem 722 (3)

Cable chain 722 (3)

Cable chain 3064 (3)

Stem 722 (3)
Two rows, back to back

Stem 3064 (3)
Two rows, back to back

Leaping hare chair pad

HARES BOUNDING ACROSS KITCHEN CHAIRS

Hares and rabbits are common sights in rural areas and these are stylised versions filled with isolated stitches arranged into patterns, from a grid of running stitch to a scattering of knots. Take your time transferring the design as the placement of the stitches is fairly important in creating the repeat patterns.

The addition of thick white piping adds a touch of sophistication to the chair pad as well as a crispness around the edges that keeps it looking fresh and modern.

Fabric
- 0.5m (20 inches) green cotton
- 50 x 50cm (20 x 20 inches) cotton voile backing fabric

Thread
DMC six-stranded cotton thread:
- Blanc White
- 3348 Light yellow green
- 472 Ultra light avocado green

Needles
Embroidery: size 7, 9
Milliner: size 8

Other
- Quilters' batting
- 2m (6½ feet) thick white piping
- Sewing thread to match

To make bigger knots, increase the number of thread strands rather than wraps around the needle, to keep them neat.

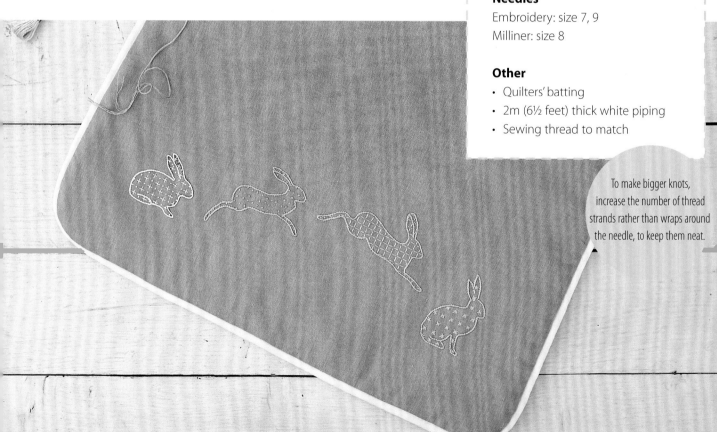

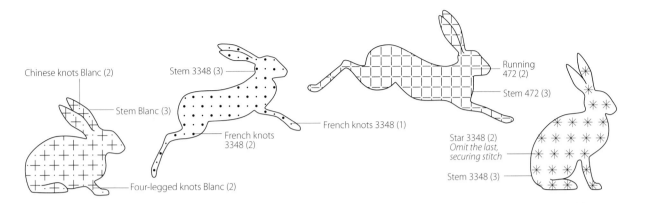

Chinese knots Blanc (2)

Stem Blanc (3)

Four-legged knots Blanc (2)

Stem 3348 (3)

French knots
3348 (2)

French knots 3348 (1)

Running
472 (2)

Stem 472 (3)

Star 3348 (2)
*Omit the last,
securing stitch*

Stem 3348 (3)

prepare

- Create a template of your chair seat by tracing it onto paper. Add a 1.2cm (½ inch) seam allowance and mark your pattern to show where the ties should be attached. Cut a 50 x 50cm (20 x 20 inch) square of green fabric.

transfer

- Transfer the cutting lines and tie positioning marks from your chair seat template onto the square of fabric, then centre the embroidery design across the bottom using one of the methods given on page 17. Overlock or tack the cotton voile to the back.

embroider

- Embroider the design according to the instructions.
- Place the fabric face down on a towel and iron the embroidery from the back. Iron the rest of the fabric, avoiding the embroidered section.

cut

- Check that the traced-on cutting lines haven't distorted during stitching and redraw them if necessary, then cut out the embroidered panel along the cutting lines.
- Use the top as a template to cut out the back of the chair pad and two pieces of quilters' batting.
- Cut four 6.5 x 25cm (2½ x 10 inch) strips of green fabric.

sew

- For the ties: Stitch a 1.2cm (½ inch) hem into one end of each fabric strip and then stitch in half lengthways using a 0.6cm (¼ inch) seam. Press the seam open and turn the right way round (attaching a safety pin to one end and then passing it through the tube is an easy way to do this). Position the seam so it runs down the centre of the strip and press flat. Stitch the hemmed end closed with a second row of stitching alongside the first.
- Sew the piping to the right side of the embroidered chair pad, 1.2cm (½ inch) from the edge. Use the zipper foot of your machine to stitch as close to the piping as possible. Start in the centre of the top edge. Cross the two ends of piping over each other neatly when you get back to the start point in such a way that the loose ends will be stitched into the seam.
- Line up two chair ties with the seams facing at each positioning mark and pin so the ties fall inside the chair pad. Secure with a row of stitching close to the edge of the fabric (inside the seam allowance).
- Layer the top and bottom of the chair pad, right sides facing, on top of the two pieces of batting with the embroidered panel on top. Stitch all the way around using the piping stitching as a guide (stitch over it); leave a gap between the ties for turning.
- Trim and then notch the seam at the corners to eliminate bulk, turn the chair pad the right way round and stitch the gap closed by hand.

Stitch your binding down
by machine to save time and
complement the stitching on
the ties.

Gardening tool roll

SOMETHING FOR THE GROW-YOUR-OWN SET

Bullion knots are perfect for the body of a small bee – alternate between two colours to create stripes. Likewise, detached chain is ideal for embroidering wings and pistil stitch for antennae.

The top edge of the tool roll folds down over the tools before being rolled up and secured with a knot or bow. And there are three roomy pockets inside for various tools.

Fabric
- 0.5m (20 inches) natural linen
- 46 x 50cm (18 x 20 inches) cotton voile backing fabric

Thread
DMC six-stranded cotton thread:
- 743 Medium yellow
- 414 Dark steel grey
- 744 Pale yellow
- 415 Pearl grey
- 3772 Very dark desert sand
- 3064 Desert sand

Needles
- Embroidery: size 7, 9
- Milliner: size 8

Other
- 2.5m (8 feet 2½ inches) green binding, 30mm (1 inch) wide
- Sewing thread to match

prepare
- Cut a 46 x 50cm (18 x 20 inch) piece of linen and draw a 41 x 46cm (16 x 18 inch) rectangle on it.

transfer
- Position the embroidery design in the lower right-hand corner of the rectangle using the cutting line on the design as a guide – the side of the rectangle to the right of the design should measure 46cm (18 inches). Transfer the design using one of the methods given on page 17 and then overlock or tack the cotton voile to the back of the fabric. Use the cutting line on the design to round off the four corners of the drawn-on rectangle.

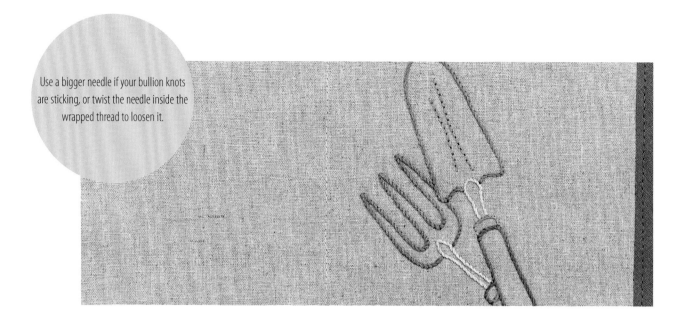

Use a bigger needle if your bullion knots are sticking, or twist the needle inside the wrapped thread to loosen it.

embroider

- Embroider the design according to the instructions. The bodies of the bees are made up of five bullion knots in 743 and 414 – alternate between the colours to create stripes and wrap your thread around the needle four to six times to create the bullions.

- Place the fabric face down on a towel and iron the embroidery from the back when done. Iron the rest of the fabric, avoiding the embroidered section, before assembling the tool roll.

cut

- Check that the cutting lines haven't distorted during stitching and redraw them if necessary, then cut out the embroidered front of the tool roll.

- Use the front as a template to cut out the lining of the bag from the remaining linen.

- Cut a 43 x 41cm (17 x 16 inch) piece of linen for the pocket.

- Cut two lengths of binding, each 30cm (12 inches).

sew

- Fold the pocket fabric in half to create a 21.5 x 41cm (8½ x 16 inch) pocket. Round off the two bottom corners using the embroidery pattern. Draw two lines on the pocket dividing it into thirds, allowing for 1.2cm (½ inch) of binding on either side.

- For the ties: Stitch a 1.2cm (½ inch) hem into one end of the binding, then fold in half lengthways and topstitch together.

- Fold the end of one tie under by 1.2cm (½ inch) and stitch to the front of the tool roll, 16cm (6¼ inches) from the left-hand edge of the fabric and 21.5cm (8½ inches) from the bottom; the loose section of the tie should lie to the left. Sew a rectangle 1.5cm (⅝ inch) wide and with a cross inside it to secure the tie.

- Pin the front of the tool roll to the lining, wrong sides facing.

- Pin the pocket to the lining of the roll, aligning the bottom edges. Stitch through all three layers along the drawn-on lines to create three tool pockets.

- Pin the seam tie to the front of the roll, 21.5cm (8½ inches) from the bottom edge and with the raw edge lining up with the raw edge of the fabric.

- Bind the edges of the roll to join the front, lining and pocket. The seam tie is secured inside the binding.

Embroidery instructions and design
Full size

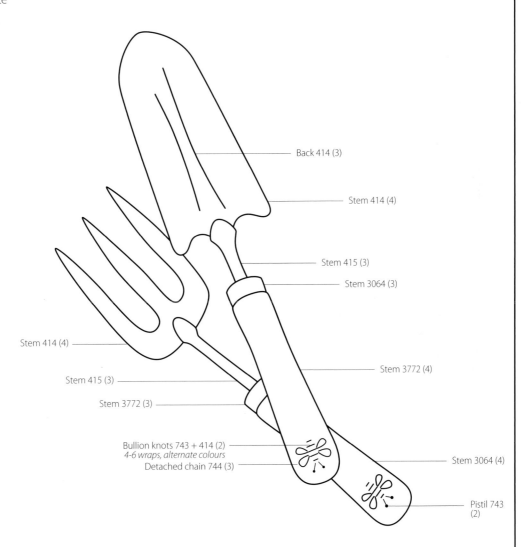

Back 414 (3)

Stem 414 (4)

Stem 415 (3)

Stem 3064 (3)

Stem 414 (4)

Stem 3772 (4)

Stem 415 (3)

Stem 3772 (3)

Bullion knots 743 + 414 (2)
4-6 wraps, alternate colours
Detached chain 744 (3)

Stem 3064 (4)

Pistil 743
(2)

Feather drawstring bag

THERE ARE ALWAYS FEATHERS
FLOATING ABOUT IN THE COUNTRY

For the embroidered feathers, intersperse your stem stitch with straight stitches when you get to the jagged bits – take your thread down, loop it around the previous stitch and come up again through the same hole to keep these points sharp.

The drawstring sleeve is sewn separately and then attached to the top of the bag at the end, so it is an easy make. Incorporating the sleeve also allows you to bring in a different fabric around the top for added detail – perfect for using up scraps of fabric.

Fabric
- 0.5m (20 inches) blue cotton
- 0.5m (20 inches) white cotton
- 25cm (10 inches) finely checked cotton
- 56 x 40cm (22 x 16 inches) cotton voile backing fabric

Thread
DMC six-stranded cotton thread:
- 3817 Light celadon green
- 3813 Light blue green
- Blanc White
- 598 Light turquoise
- 3811 Very light turquoise

Needles
Embroidery: size 7, 9
Milliner: size 8

Other
- 1.2m (3 feet 11¼ inches) thick white cord
- Sewing thread to match

Take small stitches when embroidering the downy feathers to create a fluffy effect.

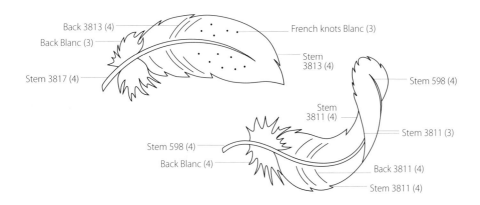

Back 3813 (4)
Back Blanc (3)
Stem 3817 (4)
French knots Blanc (3)
Stem 3813 (4)
Stem 598 (4)
Stem 3811 (4)
Stem 3811 (3)
Stem 598 (4)
Back Blanc (4)
Back 3811 (4)
Stem 3811 (4)

prepare

- Cut a 56 x 40cm (22 x 16 inch) piece of blue fabric and draw a 35 x 37cm (20¾ x 14½ inch) rectangle on it.

transfer

- Position the feather design in the lower right-hand corner of the drawn-on rectangle. Transfer the design using one of the methods given on page 17. Overlock or tack the cotton voile to the back.

embroider

- Embroider the design according to the instructions.
- Iron the embroidery face down on a towel. Iron the rest of the fabric before assembling the bag.

cut

- Check that the cutting lines haven't distorted during stitching and redraw them if necessary, then cut out the embroidered front of the bag.
- Cut a 53 x 37cm (20¾ x 14½ inch) rectangle from the remaining blue fabric for the back of the bag.
- Cut two 53 x 37cm (20¾ x 14½ inch) rectangles of white cotton for the lining.
- Cut two 9 x 72.5cm (3½ x 28½ inch) strips of the checked fabric.

sew

- Stitch a piece of white lining to the front and back of the drawstring bag – right sides facing – along the top edge using a 0.6cm (¼ inch) seam. Press the seams and then open the fabric out again.
- Pin the two pieces together right sides facing, lining on lining and bag front on bag back. Match up the stitched seams. Sew all the way around using a 0.6cm (¼ inch) seam, leaving a gap in the bottom of the lining for turning. Use a scant seam allowance for the bag and a generous one for the lining.
- Trim the corners then turn the bag the right way round through the gap and push out the blue corners – the tips of a closed pair of sewing scissors work well for this.
- Stitch the gap in the lining closed by hand and push it into the bag, lining up the bottom corners. Press the seams.
- Pin the two strips of checked fabric together, right sides facing, and stitch around the edge using a 0.6cm (¼ inch) seam. Leave a gap for turning along one of the longer sides. Turn the right way round and push out the corners, then press. Iron a 0.6cm (¼ inch) hem into the fabric on either side of the gap.
- Fold the strip in half lengthways and pin one long edge to each side of the top of the bag, overlapping by 0.6cm (¼ inch). Start on one side and work your way around to create the sleeve for the drawstring. Topstitch the sleeve to the bag, closing the gap as you go.
- Thread the cord through the sleeve so that the ends meet on one side of the bag and knot the ends together.

Butterfly cosmetic bag

A PRACTICAL ITEM EMBELLISHED WITH PURELY-FOR-PLEASURE EMBROIDERY

The butterfly features two instances of stitching over stitching: knots over back stitch and bullions over satin stitch. It's a lovely way to layer your embroidery and build up texture, as well as add detail to the design as a whole. Make sure you can still see where to place the bullions once you've satin stitched the body – make small marks along the sides of the body when tracing on your design, or use a ruler to measure the distances between bullions on the printed design and then duplicate them on your embroidery.

The grey and white patterned lining adds a surprise detail when you zip open the bag and is also a practical choice. Using a light-coloured lining makes it easier to see inside the bag but because marks from mascara or eyeliner show up more easily on lighter fabric, using a light but patterned fabric gives you the best of both worlds – marks won't show up as easily but you'll still be able to find things in the depths.

Fabric

- 35 x 50cm (14 x 20 inches) light grey linen
- 35 x 25cm (14 x 10 inches) cotton voile backing fabric
- 35 x 50cm (14 x 20 inches) patterned fabric for the lining

Thread

DMC six-stranded cotton thread:

- 169 Light pewter grey
- 775 Very light baby blue
- 3325 Light baby blue
- B5200 Snow white
- 3761 Light sky blue
- 168 Very light pewter grey

Needles

- Embroidery: size 7, 9
- Milliner: size 7, 8

Other

- 35 x 50cm (14 x 20 inches) thick iron-on stiffening (Vilene)
- 20cm (8 inch) zip, light grey
- Matching sewing thread

Use bullion knots in place of straight stitches to add more definition, substance and texture to your embroidery.

prepare

- Cut the grey linen in half into two 35 x 25cm (14 x 10 inch) pieces.

transfer

- Transfer the design onto one piece of grey linen, including the cutting lines, using one of the methods given on page 17. Overlock or tack the voile to the back of the fabric.

embroider

- Embroider the design according to the instructions.
- When the embroidery is complete, place the fabric face down on a towel and iron it from the back.

cut

- Cut out the embroidered panel along the traced-on cutting lines.
- Use the embroidered front panel as a template to cut another piece of grey linen in the same shape, as well as two from the patterned lining fabric and two more from the iron-on stiffening. Fuse the stiffening to the back of the grey fabric panels (iron on a towel again so you don't flatten the embroidery).
- Cut two 2.5 x 4cm (1 x 1½ inch) rectangles from the grey linen.

sew

- Use a 0.6cm (¼ inch) seam throughout.
- Attach the two small squares of grey linen to either end of the zip to make it fit neatly into the top of the bag. Sew the first square to the end of the zip, next to the metal crimp. The right side of the fabric should be facing down and lying over the crimp as you sew. Attach it as close to the crimp as you can (use the zipper foot of your machine to make it easier to stitch past the crimp). Open the zip halfway before stitching the second square to the other end, also right side down and so that there are 17cm (6¾ inches) between the outer raw edges of each facedown square. Fold the squares back and iron the seams flat. Trim the zip so it lines up with the folded-back fabric.
- Start constructing the bag by inserting the zip. Sandwich one side of it between one grey piece of fabric and a piece of patterned lining fabric (right sides facing) with the zip centred, facing the grey fabric and lining up with the top edges of both pieces of fabric. The squares stitched to the zip will stick out a bit. Stitch as close to the teeth of the zip as possible, using the zipper foot of your machine, as this will affect the neatness of your top corners once the bag is complete. Repeat for the other side of the zip, keeping the four fabric pieces aligned. Iron the zip seams flat and then trim the fabric squares attached to the zip to line up with the sides of the bag.
- Open the zip – you'll have to turn the bag the right way round through the zip opening later.
- Pin the two grey sides together and the two patterned sides together, right sides facing. Sew the sides of the bag: turn your fabric when you reach the zip with your needle in the down position to create a shallow V of stitching along each side of the bag. The zip falls between the two pieces of grey fabric. Stitch the bottom seams closed, but leave a gap in the patterned lining through which to turn the bag the right way round.
- To create the base of each triangular side of the bag, pull open the corner gap left unstitched as you would a bag of crisps, so that the side seam meets the bottom seam of the bag, and stitch across the corner. Repeat for the other three corners.
- Turn the bag the right way round through the gap in the lining and the open zip, and push out the corners gently with a closed pair of sewing scissors. Iron each corner for a neat finish.
- Finger press the bottom seam of the lining and stitch closed by hand using small invisible stitches. Push it into the bag, lining up the corners.

With a symmetrical design, embroider one side first to be sure you're happy with it before repeating the stitching on the other side.

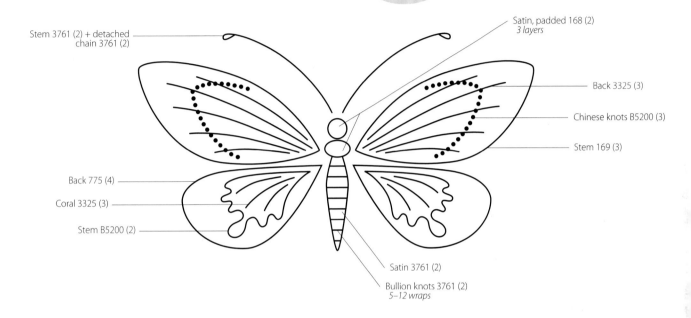

Stem 3761 (2) + detached chain 3761 (2)

Satin, padded 168 (2)
3 layers

Back 3325 (3)

Chinese knots B5200 (3)

Stem 169 (3)

Back 775 (4)

Coral 3325 (3)

Stem B5200 (2)

Satin 3761 (2)

Bullion knots 3761 (2)
5–12 wraps

Template and embroidery design

Increase by 250%

Birds

This design is more about what's not there; minimal lines create a simple depiction of two birds sitting on a branch. The use of just three stitches makes this project a quick and easy stitch.

Thread

DMC six-stranded cotton thread:

- 779 Dark cocoa
- 451 Dark shell grey
- 452 Medium shell grey
- 453 Light shell grey

Needles

- Embroidery: size 7
- Milliner: size 7, 8

Enlarge by 200%

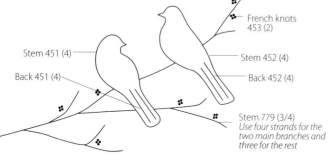

French knots 453 (2)

Stem 451 (4)

Stem 452 (4)

Back 451 (4)

Back 452 (4)

Stem 779 (3/4)
Use four strands for the two main branches and three for the rest

Dragonfly

Feather and double feather stitch are extremely well suited to insect wings as they convey lightness while filling in detail. And it's a lot easier to stitch along the traced-on lines than doing it freehand, although that comes with practice.

Thread

DMC six-stranded cotton thread:

- 989 Forest green
- 988 Medium forest green
- 598 Light turquoise
- 3811 Very light turquoise

Needles

- Embroidery: size 7
- Milliner: size 7

Enlarge by 200%

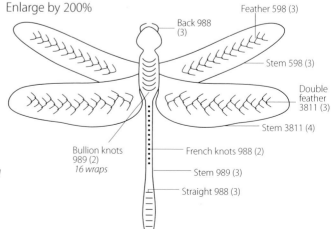

Feather 598 (3)

Back 988 (3)

Stem 598 (3)

Double feather 3811 (3)

Stem 3811 (4)

Bullion knots 989 (2)
16 wraps

French knots 988 (2)

Stem 989 (3)

Straight 988 (3)

SKILL LEVEL

Acorns

A back stitch trellis is a good way to depict the scales on acorn cups as the symmetry keeps the design contemporary. The young oak leaf is embroidered as a fly stitch leaf.

Thread

DMC six-stranded cotton thread:
- Blanc White
- 3013 Light khaki green
- 3011 Dark khaki green
- 3348 Light yellow green

Needles
- Embroidery: size 7

Enlarge by 200%

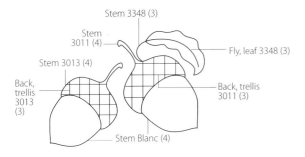

SKILL LEVEL

Mushrooms

These are fairly simple so the project is quick to stitch, with graded colour on the knot flowers to add an element of interest. Stitch the gills of the mushroom first, then outline the rest of the cap.

Thread

DMC six-stranded cotton thread:
- 3779 Ultra very light rosewood
- 309 Dark rose
- 3774 Very light desert sand
- 722 Light orange spice
- 818 Baby pink
- Blanc White
- 3064 Desert sand
- 963 Ultra very light dusty rose
- 3328 Dark salmon
- 950 Light desert sand

Needles
- Embroidery: size 7, 9
- Milliner: size 7

Enlarge by 300%

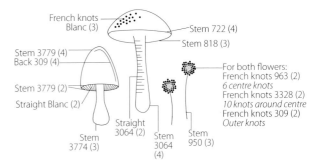

floral

An abundance of inspiration from the floral kingdom

Dog rose e-reader cover

PRACTICAL DOESN'T HAVE TO MEAN YOU FORFEIT PRETTY

Using a single strand of thread gives a delicateness that is difficult to achieve otherwise. And although I usually wrap my thread around the needle twice for French knots, here I used just one wrap for the knots on the main dog rose, in order to complement the gossamer filaments.

Use blanket stitch for flower centres, with the uprights radiating outwards.

Fabric
- 25cm (10 inches) aubergine cotton
- 25cm (10 inches) patterned cotton, for the lining
- 25cm (10 inches) cotton voile backing fabric

Thread
DMC six-stranded cotton thread:
- 3832 Raspberry
- 727 Very light topaz
- B5200 Snow white
- 3831 Dark raspberry
- 704 Bright chartreuse

Needles
- Embroidery: size 7, 9
- Milliner: size 8

Other
- Quilters' batting
- 10cm (4 inches) leather cord
- Sewing thread to match
- 1 button

French knots
B5200 (2)
1 wrap

Satin,
padded
727 (2)
3 layers

Stem 3832 (3)

Back B5200 (1)

Stem 3831 (2)

Back 727 (2)
Blanket B5200 (1)

Fly 704 (2)
*Start with a
straight stitch*

Stem 704 (2)

SKILL
LEVEL
✕

prepare

- Cut a 50 x 20cm (20 x 8 inch) piece of aubergine cotton and draw a 45 x 16cm (18 x 6¼ inch) rectangle on it. The measurements given are for a Kindle Voyage. If you have another Kindle or e-reader, measure your device first and adjust the pattern to fit. Add 1.2cm (½ inch) to the length and the width to create some space for the reader inside the cover. Then double this length and add 2cm (¾ inch) for the seam and fold allowances, plus 9.5cm (3¾ inches) for the flap, which includes a 1.2cm (½ inch) seam allowance. Add 4cm (1½ inches) to the width for the side seams and use these measurements when preparing your fabric. Position the embroidery design on the flap. The layer of batting inside the cover cushions and protects your e-reader, so it's important to add it. And as the lining fabric will show a little down the sides of the reader, it's a good idea to match it to your thread colours.

transfer

- Position the embroidery design at one end of the rectangle , on the flap of the e-reader case. Transfer the design using one of the methods given on page 17. Overlock or tack the voile to the back of the fabric.

embroider

- Embroider the design according to the instructions.
- Iron the finished embroidery face down on a towel.

cut

- Check that the drawn-on cutting lines haven't distorted during stitching and redraw them if necessary before cutting out.
- Cut a 45 x 16cm (18 x 6¼ inch) rectangle of the patterned cotton for the lining.

- Cut a 43 x 13.5cm (17 x 5¼ inch) piece of batting and round off the corners at one end.

sew

- Iron a 1.2cm (½ inch) fold into the short end of the embroidered panel (opposite the embroidery) and into one end of the patterned fabric. Unfold the hem again.
- Create a button loop with the leather cord and pin it to the front of the embroidered panel, just below the embroidery.
- Pin the embroidered panel to the lining, right sides facing and with the ironed hems lined up. Sew around three sides, leaving the folded edge unstitched and using a 1.2cm (½ inch) seam. Round off the corners closest to the embroidery and double stitch over the ends of the leather loop to secure it well. Trim the excess fabric from the rounded corners and notch them to eliminate bulk.
- Turn the e-reader cover the right way round and iron the seams flat.
- Slide the batting into the pouch, lining it up with the seams. Fold the ironed hem of the embroidered panel over the batting and the hem of the lining back into place and pin the three layers together. Topstitch the opening closed 0.6cm (¼ inch) from the edge, beginning and ending the stitching 0.6cm (¼ inch) from each side of the sleeve.
- Create a pouch by folding the bottom edge of the panel up by 17cm (6¾ inches). Pin it in place.
- Sew the sides together by machine, 0.6cm (¼ inch) from each edge.
- Fold the top, embroidered panel of the sleeve over and hand stitch a button to the front of the e-reader cover, in line with the loop.

Summer bloom placemats

FRESHEN UP THE BREAKFAST TABLE WITH VIBRANT FLORAL PLACEMATS

This project is almost a sampler because the four flowers contain a variety of interesting stitches in the petals and leaves. Some of the less commonly used ones are up and down blanket stitch, Palestrina, heavy chain and long-armed feather stitch, which are all well suited to embroidered flora.

Placemats are handy in lieu of a tablecloth and are easy to sew, too. These are designed for mixing and matching – pick your favourite design and stitch it in different colours or double up the designs for additional mats. Use fabric that washes well, as placemats tend to need regular laundering.

Fabric
- 80cm (31 inches) light, natural-coloured cotton
- 80cm (31 inches) cotton voile backing fabric
- 70cm (27 inches) dark, natural-coloured cotton

Thread
DMC six-stranded cotton thread:
- 498 Dark red
- 3832 Raspberry
- 726 Light topaz
- 703 Chartreuse
- 702 Kelly green
- 3831 Dark raspberry
- 727 Very light topaz

Needles
- Embroidery: size 7, 9
- Milliner: size 5, 7

Other
- 70cm (27 inches) lightweight iron-on stiffening (Vilene)
- Matching sewing thread

prepare
- Cut the lighter fabric into four rectangles measuring 50 x 38cm (20 x 15 inches). Do the same with the cotton voile backing fabric.

transfer
- Draw a 42 x 30.5cm (16½ x 12 inch) rectangle on each of the lighter pieces of fabric and position the designs in the bottom, right-hand corners. Transfer a design onto each placemat using one of the methods given on page 17 and overlock or tack a piece of cotton voile to the back of each.

embroider
- Embroider the designs according to the instructions.
- Once you've finished embroidering, place the fabric face down on a towel and iron the embroidery from the back. Iron the placemats, avoiding the embroidered section, before assembling them.

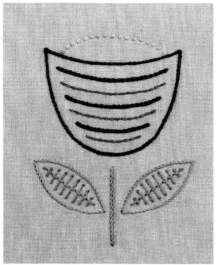

cut

- Check that the cutting lines haven't distorted during stitching and redraw them if necessary before cutting out each of the fronts of the placemats.

- Cut four 42 x 30.5cm (16½ x 12 inch) rectangles of the darker fabric for the backs.

- Cut four 42 x 30.5cm (16½ x 12 inch) rectangles of iron-on stiffening and fuse to the wrong sides of each of the backs of the placemats with a hot iron.

sew

- Pin the fronts to the backs, right sides facing.

- Stitch around all four edges by machine with a 0.6cm (¼ inch) seam, rotating your fabric with the needle in the down position at the corners. Leave about a 10cm (4 inch) gap along the edge opposite the embroidery for turning.

- Trim the corners to reduce bulk and turn the placemats the right way round through the gap. Push the corners out neatly (and gently) with a closed pair of sewing scissors or other suitable tool.

- Iron the seams flat and press a 0.6cm (¼ inch) hem into the fabric on either side of the gap to form a straight edge.

- Stitch the gap closed by hand, using small invisible stitches.

Use stitches you can easily adjust the width of to fill leaves, such as pistil, blanket stitch variations and Palestrina.

Embroidery instructions and designs

Enlarge by 200%

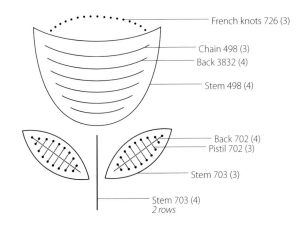

French knots 726 (3)

Chain 498 (3)
Back 3832 (4)

Stem 498 (4)

Back 702 (4)
Pistil 702 (3)

Stem 703 (3)

Stem 703 (4)
2 rows

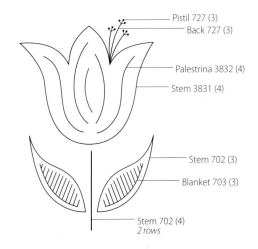

Pistil 727 (3)
Back 727 (3)

Palestrina 3832 (4)

Stem 3831 (4)

Stem 702 (3)

Blanket 703 (3)

Stem 702 (4)
2 rows

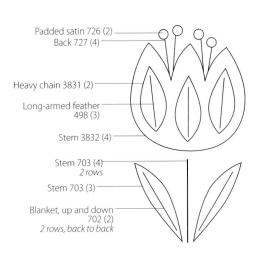

Padded satin 726 (2)
Back 727 (4)

Heavy chain 3831 (2)

Long-armed feather
498 (3)

Stem 3832 (4)

Stem 703 (4)
2 rows

Stem 703 (3)

Blanket, up and down
702 (2)
2 rows, back to back

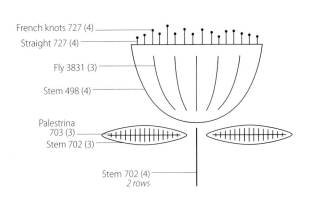

French knots 727 (4)
Straight 727 (4)

Fly 3831 (3)

Stem 498 (4)

Palestrina
703 (3)
Stem 702 (3)

Stem 702 (4)
2 rows

Fabric

- 38 x 48cm (15 x 19 inches) light, natural-coloured cotton
- 38 x 48cm (15 x 19 inches) cotton voile backing fabric

Thread

DMC six-stranded cotton thread:

- 3041 Medium antique violet
- 3743 Very light antique violet
- 304 Medium red
- B5200 Snow white
- 760 Salmon
- 702 Kelly green
- 704 Bright chartreuse
- 703 Chartreuse
- 772 Very light yellow green
- 726 Light topaz
- 727 Very light topaz
- 725 Medium light topaz
- 3831 Dark raspberry
- 761 Light salmon
- 3740 Dark antique violet
- 3042 Light antique violet
- 3832 Medium raspberry

Needles

- Embroidery: size 7, 9
- Milliner: size 5, 7, 8

Other

- Foam board
- Sewing thread to match
- Frame, made to fit

Growing wild wall art

STITCH AN INFORMAL GARDEN FOR YOUR WALL

Flowers and embroidery were made to pair up. The variety of surface embroidery stitches that can be used to create petals, stamens, leaves and stems make floral designs probably the most fun to embroider.

Get your finished work framed professionally or buy a frame that'll work for the design and cut your fabric to fit. If you are going down the professional route, ask your framer to use non-reflective glass so your embroidery is more visible.

transfer

- Centre the floral wall art design on the cotton fabric and transfer using one of the methods given on page 17. Overlock or tack the cotton voile to the back of the fabric.

embroider

- Embroider the design according to the instructions.
- Place the embroidered fabric face down on a towel and iron it well from the back.

mount

- Cut a 28 x 37cm (11 x 14½ inch) rectangle of foam board.
- Centre the embroidered fabric on top of the board and pin it in place by sticking pins through the fabric and into the sides of the board. Smooth the fabric over the edges of the board as you pin.
- Turn it over and fold opposite sides of the fabric over the board. Use a long piece of sewing thread and make small stitches in first the top, then bottom fabric to create a zigzag pattern – you're lacing the fabric to hold it in place. Pull the thread taut before securing the end, taking care not to bend the board. Do the same with the remaining sides.
- Frame the work as desired.

Space knots differently to create various flower centres – fill one centre completely to create a solid area of embroidery, space knots randomly in a circular shape for another and dot the knots evenly to create a pattern inside a third.

Embroidery design
Enlarge by 250%

Embroidery instructions

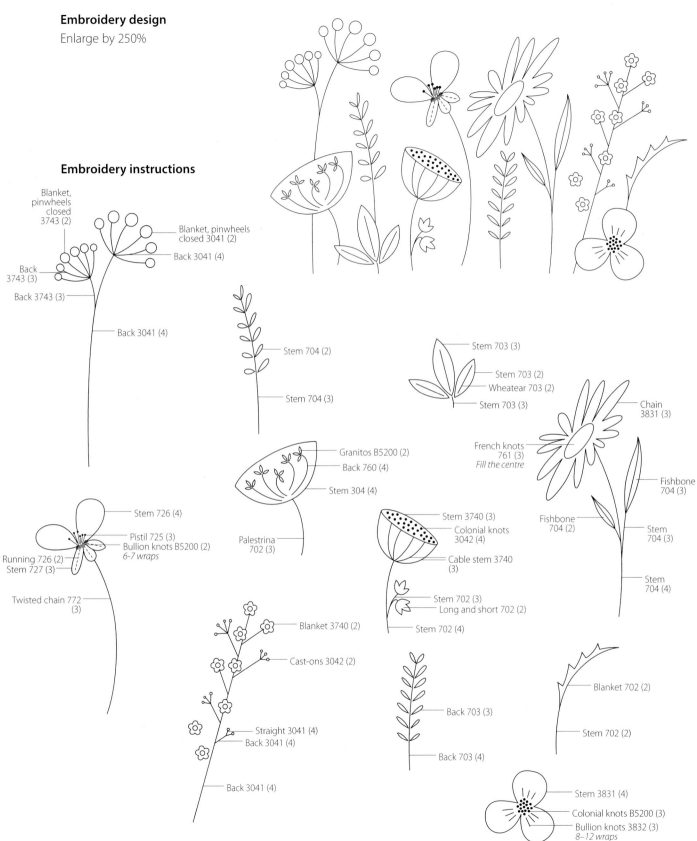

Blanket, pinwheels closed 3743 (2)

Blanket, pinwheels closed 3041 (2)

Back 3041 (4)

Back 3743 (3)

Back 3743 (3)

Back 3041 (4)

Stem 704 (2)

Stem 704 (3)

Stem 703 (3)

Stem 703 (2)

Wheatear 703 (2)

Stem 703 (3)

Chain 3831 (3)

Granitos B5200 (2)

Back 760 (4)

Stem 304 (4)

French knots 761 (3)
Fill the centre

Fishbone 704 (3)

Stem 726 (4)

Pistil 725 (3)

Bullion knots B5200 (2)
6-7 wraps

Running 726 (2)

Stem 727 (3)

Twisted chain 772 (3)

Palestrina 702 (3)

Stem 3740 (3)

Colonial knots 3042 (4)

Cable stem 3740 (3)

Fishbone 704 (2)

Stem 704 (3)

Stem 704 (4)

Stem 702 (3)

Long and short 702 (2)

Stem 702 (4)

Blanket 3740 (2)

Cast-ons 3042 (2)

Straight 3041 (4)

Back 3041 (4)

Back 703 (3)

Back 703 (4)

Blanket 702 (2)

Stem 702 (2)

Back 3041 (4)

Stem 3831 (4)

Colonial knots B5200 (3)

Bullion knots 3832 (3)
8-12 wraps

Rambling pillowcases

DELICATE LEAVES AND BLOSSOMS ON CLIMBING VINES

The long-armed feather stitch vine is a good example of adapting a stitch to suit your needs, as it has to be stitched in sets of three stitches to achieve the desired look. Alternating blanket stitch is an unusual variation that works to great effect as a climbing creeper, but it also looks equally good as the veins of a leaf.

The measurements given are for a standard-size pillowcase, but measure your pillows first and adjust the pattern if necessary to fit. Use cotton fabric as it'll be comfortable to sleep on and will wash well.

Embroider onto ready-made pillowcases. It'll be trickier to reach the back of your work but it eliminates any sewing.

prepare

- Cut the cotton in half lengthways and draw a 45 x 158cm (17½ x 62 inch) rectangle on each piece. Draw positioning marks 79cm (31 inches) from one end of the pillowcase.

transfer

- Position each of the embroidery designs between the positioning marks on each pillowcase and transfer using one of the methods given on page 17. White dressmakers' carbon works well on darker-coloured fabric.

embroider

- Embroider the design according to the instructions.
- Iron the embroidered sections of each pillowcase face down on a towel and iron the rest of the pillowcase, avoiding the embroidered section, before beginning to sew.

cut

- Check that the cutting lines haven't distorted during stitching and redraw them if necessary, then cut out the pillowcases.

sew

- Stitch a 1.2cm (½ inch) double-fold hem into the shorter sides of each pillowcase and press.
- With the wrong side of the embroidery facing up, pin a 15cm (6 inch) fold into the short edge towards the left of the embroidered design, then fold the pillowcase in half, right sides facing, and pin the side seams together.
- Stitch the sides together using a 0.6cm (¼ inch) seam and overlock or zigzag the raw edges.
- Remove the tacking holding the cotton voile backing fabric in place and press the seams.

Keep your fabric taut in your hoop and watch your tension when embroidering a larger design with six strands of thread, to keep your stitching from pulling too tight or sagging.

 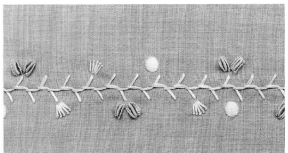

Embroidery instructions

Embroidery designs
Enlarge by 300%

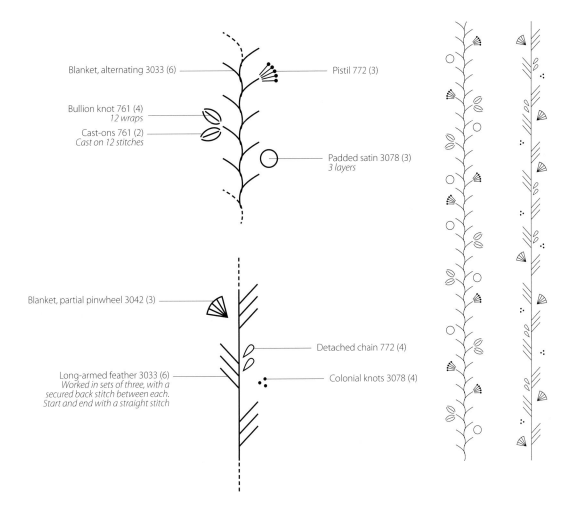

Blanket, alternating 3033 (6)

Pistil 772 (3)

Bullion knot 761 (4)
12 wraps

Cast-ons 761 (2)
Cast on 12 stitches

Padded satin 3078 (3)
3 layers

Blanket, partial pinwheel 3042 (3)

Detached chain 772 (4)

Long-armed feather 3033 (6)
*Worked in sets of three, with a
secured back stitch between each.
Start and end with a straight stitch*

Colonial knots 3078 (4)

Insect key fobs

IDENTIFY KEYS WITH A TOUCH OF HAND STITCHING

The detached chain stitch butterflies are really easy to embroider, but the dragonfly is a little more involved. Long bullion knots are easier to create with fewer strands of thread, so the body of the dragonfly is made up of two bullions rather than a single, fatter one.

This is a good project for using up scraps of fabric – solid colours for the fronts and bits of patterned fabric for the back. Turning the key fobs the right way round can be a bit fiddly – a crochet hook or similar tool will help smooth the seams of the fob into shape.

Fabric
- 20 x 20cm (8 x 8 inch) white cotton
- 20 x 20cm (8 x 8 inch) yellow cotton
- Two 20 x 20cm (8 x 8 inch) squares cotton voile backing fabric
- 15 x 10cm (6 x 4 inch) green cotton
- 15 x 10cm (6 x 4 inch) patterned cotton

Thread
DMC six-stranded cotton thread:
- 726 Light topaz
- 772 Very light yellow green
- 703 Chartreuse
- 3833 Light raspberry
- 3832 Medium raspberry
- 3041 Medium antique violet

Needles
- Embroidery: size 7, 9
- Milliner: size 5, 8

Other
- Thick iron-on stiffening (Vilene)
- Two key rings, 30mm (1 inch) in diameter
- Sewing thread, to match

SKILL
LEVEL

✕ ✕

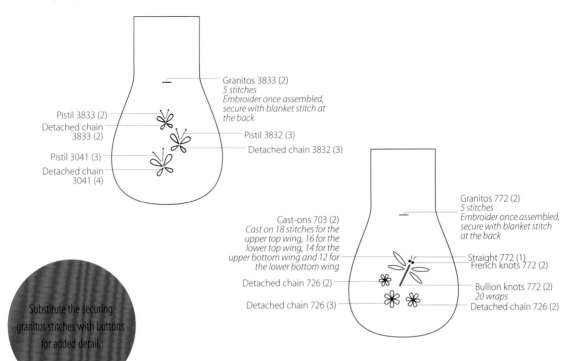

Granitos 3833 (2)
5 stitches
Embroider once assembled,
secure with blanket stitch at
the back

Pistil 3833 (2)
Detached chain
3833 (2)

Pistil 3041 (3)
Detached chain
3041 (4)

Pistil 3832 (3)
Detached chain 3832 (3)

Cast-ons 703 (2)
Cast on 18 stitches for the
upper top wing, 16 for the
lower top wing, 14 for the
upper bottom wing and 12 for
the lower bottom wing

Detached chain 726 (2)

Detached chain 726 (3)

Granitos 772 (2)
5 stitches
Embroider once assembled,
secure with blanket stitch
at the back

Straight 772 (1)
French knots 772 (2)

Bullion knots 772 (2)
20 wraps
Detached chain 726 (2)

Substitute the securing granitos stitches with buttons for added detail.

transfer

- Transfer the dragonfly design onto the square of white cotton and the three butterflies onto the yellow fabric using one of the methods given on page 17. Include cutting lines.

embroider

- Embroider the designs according to the instructions.
- When done, place the embroidery face down on a towel and iron the back.

cut

- Check that the cutting lines haven't distorted during stitching and redraw them if necessary, then cut out the embroidered fronts.
- Use the fronts of the key fobs as templates to cut out two pieces of thick stiffening, a green back and a patterned back.

sew

- Fuse the stiffening to the wrong side of the key fob front, ironing on a towel to prevent the embroidery from being squashed flat.
- Line up the front and back of the fob, right sides facing, and stitch together by machine using a 0.6cm (¼ inch) seam. Leave the 'neck' of the fob open and notch/clip the seams where they curve to eliminate bulk, taking care not to cut the seam stitching.
- Turn the right way round. Fold the top of the neck over on itself and roll the bottom half of the fob into a tube, then pull it through the neck bit by bit. Use a crochet hook or similar tool to push out the seams gently so you get an even shape and press flat.
- Finger press a 0.6cm (¼ inch) seam into the opening and stitch closed by hand with small invisible stitching.
- Fold the neck over the key ring and stitch in place where indicated with a granitos stitch.

Spring wreath

A CIRCLE OF SPRIGS AND BLOOMS

This design incorporates a host of stitches, from couching to coral and cast-on stitch – and three different ways to do satin stitch. It's a project that you can pick up and put down again regularly, working your way through it leaf by leaf, flower by flower.

Frame your finished wreath. It's the perfect size for hanging in a nook or narrow section of wall.

Fabric
- 40 x 40cm (16 x 16 inch) green cotton
- 40 x 40cm (16 x 16 inch) cotton voile backing fabric

Thread
DMC six-stranded cotton thread:
- 3740 Dark antique violet
- 3041 Medium antique violet
- 3832 Medium raspberry
- 3831 Dark raspberry
- 414 Dark steel grey
- 415 Pearl grey
- B5200 Snow white
- 726 Light topaz
- 703 Chartreuse
- 3078 Very light golden yellow
- 727 Very light topaz

Needles
- Embroidery: size 7, 9
- Milliner: size 5, 7

Fill larger areas of padded satin stitch with chain stitch rather than satin. It is a bulkier stitch and will raise your satin stitching higher.

SKILL
LEVEL

✕ ✕ ✕

Satin 415 (2)
Stem 414 (4)
Stem 727 (4)
Chain 726 (2)
Stem 703 (3)
Arrowhead 703 (2)
Back 703 (4)
Stem 3831 (3)
Chinese knots B5200 (3)
Straight 3832 (2)
Stem 414 (4)
Coral 414 (3) + 415 (2)
Stem 414 (2)
Chain 3831 (4)
Couching 3831 (4) + 3832 (2)
Blanket 3832 (2)
Chinese knots 3831 (2)

Heavy chain 3740 (3)
Padded satin 3041 (2)
Pad with chain stitch
Stem 3832 (3)
Stem 3831 (3)
Colonial knots 3831 (3)
Blanket B5200 (3)
Chinese knots 726 (2)
Chain 703 (3)
Back 703 (4)
Colonial knots 703 (4)
Back 703 (4)
Stem 3740 (3)
Cast-on 3041 (2)
*Cast on 6–10 stitches.
Catch each one down with a
small straight stitch over the
'bar' of one of the cast-on
stitches, so they lie flat*
Back 726 (4)
Blanket 727 (2)
Padded satin 3078 (2)

transfer

- Transfer the wreath design onto the cotton using one of the methods given on page 17.

embroider

- Embroider the design according to the instructions.
- When complete, place the fabric face down on a towel and iron from the back.

Buck

STRAIGHT OUT OF THE WILD

Grouping the thread colours creates impact and gives the design a modern feel.

SKILL LEVEL ✕ ✕

Thread

DMC six-stranded cotton thread:

- 703 Chartreuse
- 726 Light topaz
- B5200 Snow white
- 3831 Dark raspberry

Needles

- Embroidery: size 7, 9
- Milliner: size 7

Enlarge by 250%

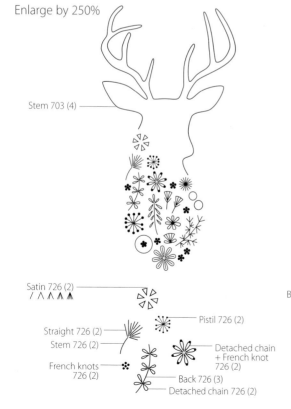

Stem 703 (4)

Satin 726 (2)

Straight 726 (2)
Stem 726 (2)
French knots 726 (2)

Pistil 726 (2)

Detached chain + French knot 726 (2)

Back 726 (3)
Detached chain 726 (2)

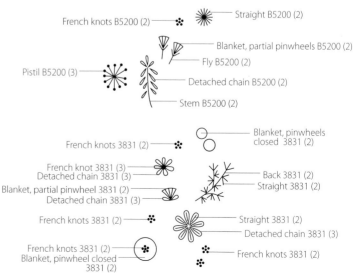

French knots B5200 (2)

Straight B5200 (2)

Blanket, partial pinwheels B5200 (2)

Fly B5200 (2)

Pistil B5200 (3)

Detached chain B5200 (2)

Stem B5200 (2)

French knots 3831 (2)

Blanket, pinwheels closed 3831 (2)

French knot 3831 (3)
Detached chain 3831 (3)

Back 3831 (2)
Straight 3831 (2)

Blanket, partial pinwheel 3831 (2)
Detached chain 3831 (3)

French knots 3831 (2)

Straight 3831 (2)
Detached chain 3831 (3)

French knots 3831 (2)
Blanket, pinwheel closed 3831 (2)

French knots 3831 (2)

SKILL LEVEL ✗

Butterfly

VINTAGE-INSPIRED STITCHING ON VIBRANT WINGS

Delicate lazy daisy flowers are common in vintage embroidery, but incorporating them into a more modern design and using bolder colour threads than would have been used then gives them a contemporary feel.

Enlarge by 250%

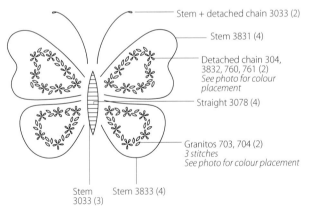

Stem + detached chain 3033 (2)

Stem 3831 (4)

Detached chain 304, 3832, 760, 761 (2)
See photo for colour placement

Straight 3078 (4)

Granitos 703, 704 (2)
3 stitches
See photo for colour placement

Stem 3033 (3)

Stem 3833 (4)

Thread
DMC six-stranded cotton thread:
- 3078 Very light golden yellow
- 3033 Very light mocha brown
- 3831 Dark raspberry
- 3833 Light raspberry
- 304 Medium red
- 3832 Medium raspberry
- 760 Salmon
- 761 Light salmon
- 703 Chartreuse
- 704 Bright chartreuse

Needles
- Embroidery: size 7, 9
- Milliner: size 5, 7

121

vintage

A retro, mid-century take on

yesteryear

Needlebook

A CHEERFUL PLACE TO STASH YOUR PINS AND NEEDLES

Blanket stitch was extremely popular in bygone years and this design features blanket stitch pinwheels with both open and closed centres.

Needlebooks were once a staple of every sewing basket and are still handy for keeping embroidery needles in order, especially if you use a lot of different types of needles. This needlebook has four leaves or pages, but you could add a couple more if you preferred.

Fabric
- 30 x 25cm (12 x 10 inches) red cotton
- 30 x 25cm (12 x 10 inches) cotton voile backing fabric
- 30 x 25cm (12 x 10 inches) pink cotton

Thread
DMC six-stranded cotton thread:
- 3712 Medium salmon
- 3713 Very light salmon
- 726 Light topaz
- 3348 Light yellow green

Needles
- Embroidery: size 7, 9

Other
- White felt
- Matching sewing thread

To create a sharp leaf tip in chain stitch, secure the last chain in the row and then come up inside this chain stitch when starting to embroider down the other side of the leaf.

Chinese knots 3712 (2)
Stem 3712 (2)
Blanket, pinwheel closed 3713 (2)
Blanket, pinwheel open 726 (2)
Stem 3348 (2)
Fly 3348 (2)
Chain 3348 (2)
Fly 3348 (2)
Chain 3348 (3)
Stem 3348 (3)
Stem 3713 (4)
Blanket, pinwheel open 3712 (3)
Blanket, pinwheel open 726 (2)
Blanket, pinwheel open 3713 (2)
Stem 3712 (3)

transfer

- Draw a 24 x 13cm (9½ x 5 inch) rectangle on the red fabric and centre the embroidery design in the right-hand half. Transfer using one of the methods given on page 17. Overlock or tack the cotton voile to the back.

embroider

- Embroider the design according to the instructions.
- Iron face down on a towel when complete.

cut

- Check that the cutting lines haven't distorted during stitching and redraw them if necessary before cutting out the needlebook front.
- Cut a 24 x 13cm (9½ x 5 inch) rectangle from the pink fabric.
- Cut two 21 x 9.5cm (8¼ x 3¾ inch) pieces of felt.

sew

- Pin the needlebook front to the pink lining fabric, right sides facing, and stitch all the way around using a 0.6cm (¼ inch) seam. Leave a gap for turning along the bottom edge.
- Trim the corners and turn the right way round. Push the corners out neatly (a closed pair of sewing scissors works well for this) and press the seams. Iron a 0.6cm (¼ inch) hem into the fabric on either side of the gap and then stitch closed by hand.
- Centre the two pieces of felt on top of the lining and pin in place. Flip the needlebook over and stitch through all three layers to form the spine. Match the thread on your bobbin to the felt, so the stitching matches the fabric on the outside and the felt on the inside. Begin and end the row of stitching so it just catches the felt down, rather than from edge to edge.
- Fold in half along the spine and finger press so the needlebook stays closed.

Bird coin purse

INSPIRED BY WOODEN TOY BIRDS

Clasp purses are the ideal size for small embroidery designs, you can make them in a day and they're useful for carting about and storing much more than just coins. The little fellow on this one could be stitched in a single colour thread for a more illustrative rendering. The dotty lining fabric adds to the quirkiness of this design.

Create a purse pattern to fit your clasp by drawing around the outside of the clasp first and then sketching the rest of the purse shape below it. Add a seam allowance and place your stitch markings about 1.2cm (½ inch) below the purse hinge.

Go through your fabric scraps to find small pieces for this project – it uses so little. Just make sure the piece you use for the front of the purse is big enough to fit in an embroidery hoop.

Fabric

- 25 x 40cm (10 x 16 inches) blue cotton
- 25 x 25cm (10 x 10 inches) cotton voile backing fabric
- 30 x 15cm (12 x 6 inches) black and white dot fabric

Thread

DMC six-stranded cotton thread:

- 726 Light topaz
- 3811 Very light turquoise
- 310 Black
- 3849 Light teal green
- B5200 Snow white
- 3347 Medium yellow green
- 347 Very dark salmon

Needles

- Embroidery: size 7, 9

Other

- Clasp purse frame
- Strong glue
- Matching sewing thread

Embroider the beak before stitching the head of the bird to avoid your needle getting caught up in the embroidery.

Template, embroidery instructions and design

Enlarge by 150%

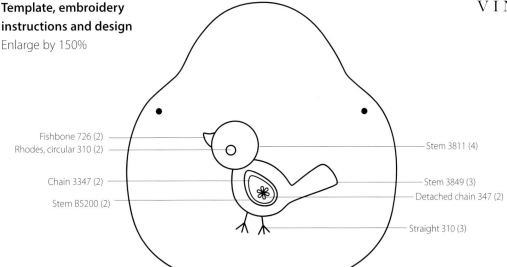

Fishbone 726 (2)
Rhodes, circular 310 (2)
Chain 3347 (2)
Stem B5200 (2)

Stem 3811 (4)
Stem 3849 (3)
Detached chain 347 (2)
Straight 310 (3)

prepare

- Cut a 25 x 25cm (10 x 10 inch) square of blue fabric.

transfer

- Position the purse design on the blue square of fabric using one of the methods given on page 17. Include the cutting lines and stitch markings. Overlock or tack the cotton voile to the back.

embroider

- Embroider the design according to the instructions.
- Lay the fabric face down on a towel and iron from the back.

cut

- Check that the cutting lines haven't distorted during stitching and redraw them if necessary before cutting out the purse front.
- Use the template to cut out the back of the purse, plus two pieces of black and white dot lining fabric. Include the stitch markings.

sew

- Stitch the embroidered purse front to the purse back, starting at one stitch marking and stitching down the side, along the bottom and back up the other side to the opposite stitch marking. Use a 0.6cm (¼ inch) seam.

- Sew the lining in the same way, but leave a turning gap in the bottom seam.

- Slip the purse into the lining with the purse turned the right way round; the right sides of the fabric should be facing.

- Sew the lining to each purse flap from one stitch marking, going up the side, along the top and down the other side. Start and end where your original side seams start and end.

- Notch the curved seams of the purse and then turn the right way round through the gap in the lining. Push the lining into the purse and press the seams neatly, then stitch the gap closed by hand.

- Optional: stick a piece of masking tape along the top edges of the purse to stop the glue used to secure the purse clasp frame spreading onto the fabric. Remove it once the frame is in place.

- Attach the purse to the frame one side at a time. Apply a generous amount of glue to the inside of the frame and the exposed edge of the fabric. Start at the hinges and push the fabric into the frame with a small pair of scissors or similarly sharp tool so that the blue fabric is up against the frame. Work your way to the centre clasp from either side. Check that the lining is also even inside the frame. Allow the glue to dry for a little while and then do the same for the other flap of the purse.

Glasses pouch

A QUICK AND EASY, HIS AND HERS PROJECT

Protect the lenses of your glasses and sunglasses from scratches with a bit of retro flair. These two pairs of 'glasses' don't take long at all to embroider, and the sewing part of the project is quick and easy too.

The pouches are padded with quilters' batting and have an opening at one end for easy access. This is especially handy if you find yourself switching between pairs of glasses or swopping sunglasses for glasses on a regular basis.

Fabric
- 20cm (8 inches) yellow cotton
- 20cm (8 inches) grey-brown cotton
- Two 30 x 20cm (12 x 8 inch) pieces cotton voile backing fabric
- 20cm (8 inches) green and white dot cotton
- 20cm (8 inches) floral patterned cotton

Thread
DMC six-stranded cotton thread:
- 347 Very dark salmon
- 3712 Medium salmon
- 743 Medium yellow
- 3346 Hunter green
- B5200 Snow white

Needles
- Embroidery: size 7

Other
- Quilters' batting
- Matching sewing thread

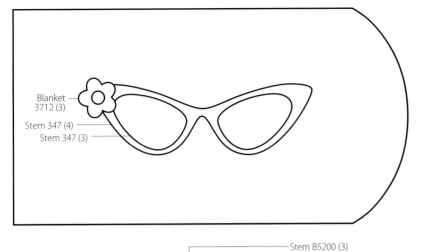

Blanket 3712 (3)

Stem 347 (4)

Stem 347 (3)

Stem B5200 (3)

Back 743 (4)

Stem 3346 (4)
Stem 3346 (3)

SKILL LEVEL

✕

prepare

• Cut two 30 x 20cm (12 x 8 inch) pieces of fabric – one yellow, the other grey-brown.

transfer

• Transfer the red glasses outline onto the yellow fabric and the green glasses onto the grey-brown fabric using one of the methods given on page 17, including the cutting lines (for the green glasses, use the same cutting lines given for the red glasses template). Overlock or tack a piece of cotton voile to the back of each.

embroider

• Embroider the designs according to the instructions.

• Iron the embroidered pouch fronts face down on a towel.

cut

• Check that the cutting lines haven't distorted during stitching and redraw them if necessary before cutting out the fronts of the pouches.

• Use the front as a template. Cut a back, two pieces of lining and two pieces of batting for each pouch.

sew

• For each pouch, sew a piece of batting and lining to the front and back along the top curved edge using a 0.6cm (¼ inch) seam. Layer the fabric by starting with a piece of batting, then placing the front/back on top of this with the embroidery/right side facing up and then putting the lining on top with the right side of the fabric facing down. Cut notches into the seam allowance to eliminate bulk, flip the lining over and press the seam.

• Open out the fabric again and pin the front to the back and the two pieces of lining together. Keep the batting with the front/back of the pouch.

• Sew around the edges using a generous 0.6cm (¼ inch) seam for the lining and a scant 0.6cm (¼ inch) seam for the pouch. Leave a gap in the bottom of the lining for turning.

• Trim the corners and turn the right way round. Push the corners out neatly – a closed pair of sewing scissors works well for this – and press the seams.

• Stitch the lining closed by hand and push it into the pouch. Press the seams again lightly.

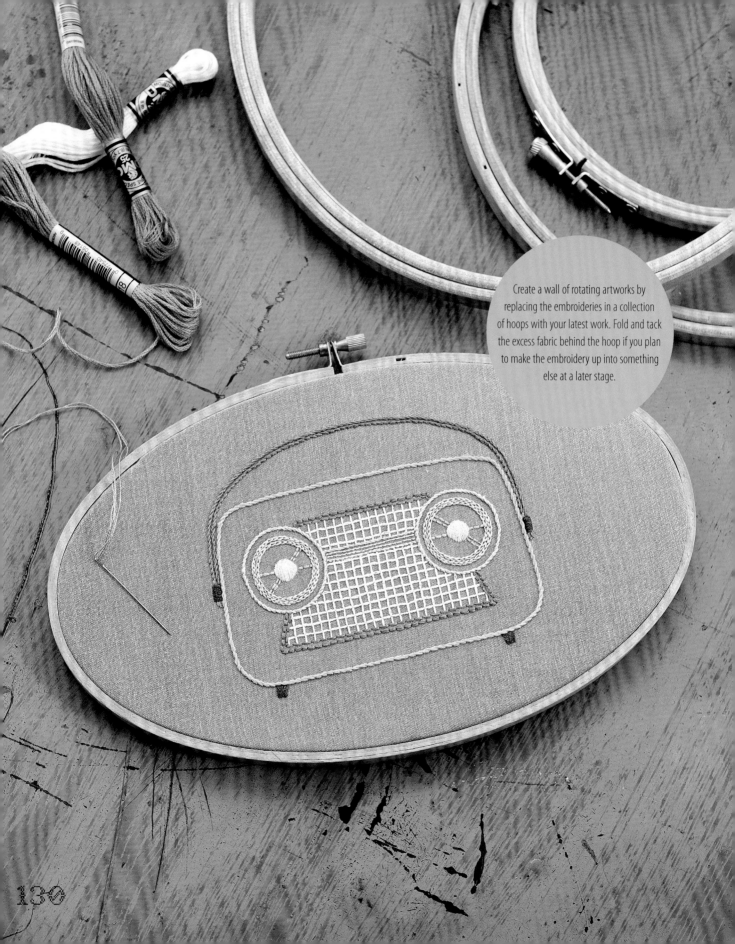

Create a wall of rotating artworks by replacing the embroideries in a collection of hoops with your latest work. Fold and tack the excess fabric behind the hoop if you plan to make the embroidery up into something else at a later stage.

Radio hoop art

A READY-MADE FRAME FOR EMBROIDERED ART

The back stitch trellis of this design takes a little while to embroider but the stitch is so well suited to a radio speaker that it's worth the extra minutes. And the bright colours make for cheerful stitching sessions.

Embroidery hoops are a quick and easy way of hanging embroidered wall art and are naturally well suited to the medium. Keep an eye out for vintage wooden hoops in second-hand and charity shops, and adjust the size of the fabric to fit your particular hoop.

Fabric
- 30 x 25cm (12 x 10 inches) blue-grey cotton
- 30 x 25cm (12 x 10 inches) cotton voile backing fabric

Thread
DMC six-stranded cotton thread:
- B5200 Snow white
- 3843 Electric blue
- 954 Nile green
- 726 Light topaz
- 3846 Light bright turquoise
- 779 Dark cocoa

Needles
- Embroidery: size 7, 9

Other
- Oval embroidery hoop, 23cm (9 inches) wide
- Matching sewing thread

Although the occasional split is inevitable, try to avoid splitting the thread when embroidering a back stitch trellis – using a stab stitch technique will help.

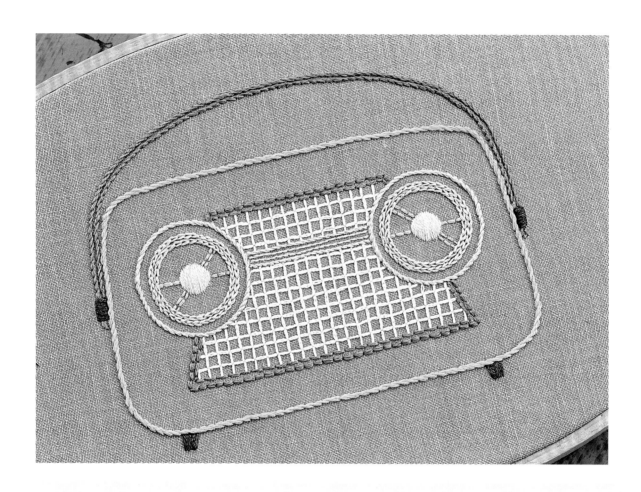

transfer

- Transfer the radio design onto the blue-grey fabric using one of the methods given on page 17 and overlock or tack the cotton voile to the back.

embroider

- Embroider the design according to the instructions.
- When you've finished embroidering, place the fabric face down on a towel and iron the back of the work.

Embroidery instructions and design
Full size

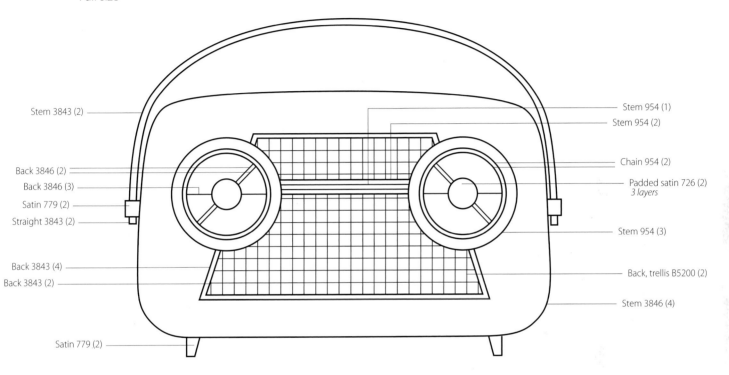

Stem 3843 (2)

Stem 954 (1)

Stem 954 (2)

Chain 954 (2)

Back 3846 (2)

Back 3846 (3)

Satin 779 (2)

Straight 3843 (2)

Padded satin 726 (2)
3 layers

Stem 954 (3)

Back 3843 (4)

Back 3843 (2)

Back, trellis B5200 (2)

Stem 3846 (4)

Satin 779 (2)

sew

- Position the embroidered design in the hoop so it lies in the centre.

- Cut away the excess fabric, about 2.5cm (1 inch) from the edge of the hoop.

- Remove the fabric from the hoop and overlock or zigzag the edge to keep it from fraying.

- Place the embroidery back in the hoop and hand stitch a row of running stitches around the edge of the fabric with sewing thread, leaving a long tail at either end.

- Use the tails of thread to gather the fabric, pulling it behind the hoop. Knot the thread to secure the gathering and your hoop art is ready to hang.

Kitchen scale apron

A REVERSIBLE APRON MADE FOR BAKING

Palestrina stitch was the obvious choice for the gauge of the kitchen scale. Keep the knots close together and adjust the length of the 'arms' of each stitch to create the measurements on the gauge.

Use a few different fabrics for the various parts of the apron but try to choose those with a common colour or two – I've gone with red and turquoise. And match your embroidery threads for the kitchen scale design to the fabric for consistency. Use another fabric on the back for two completely different looks, or add a pocket.

Fabric
- 75cm (30 inches) light turquoise cotton
- 69 x 43cm (27 x 17 inches) cotton voile backing fabric
- 25cm (10 inches) patterned cotton
- 25cm (10 inches) red and white dot cotton

Thread
DMC six-stranded cotton thread:
- 3033 Very light mocha brown
- 779 Dark cocoa
- 347 Very dark salmon
- 743 Medium yellow
- Blanc White

Needles
- Embroidery: size 7, 9

Other
- 2m (6½ feet) red binding, 12mm (½ inch) wide
- Matching sewing thread

Two knife pleats on either side give the apron shape and fullness without creating bulk.

Patterned fabric template

Enlarge by 400%

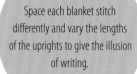

Space each blanket stitch differently and vary the lengths of the uprights to give the illusion of writing.

prepare

- Cut a 69 x 43cm (27 x 17 inch) piece of light turquoise fabric and draw a 63.5 x 37cm (25 x 14½ inch) rectangle on it. Draw positioning marks along the top of the rectangle for the pleats, at 4cm (1⅝ inches), 6.5cm (2½ inches), 13.5cm (5⅜ inches) and 16cm (6¼ inches) from the outer edge.

transfer

- Position the scale design in the lower left-hand corner of the drawn-on rectangle – 13cm (5 inches) from the side and 6.5cm (2½ inches) from the bottom of the rectangle – using one of the methods given on page 17, then overlock or tack the cotton voile to the back.

embroider

- Embroider the design according to the instructions.

- Press the embroidery face down on a towel and give the rest of the apron front a good iron, avoiding the embroidered section, before making it up.

cut

- Check that the cutting lines haven't distorted during stitching and redraw them if necessary before cutting out the apron front.

- Cut another 63.5 x 37cm (25 x 14½ inch) rectangle from the light turquoise fabric for the back of the apron (mark the pleat positioning as before).

- Cut two panels from the patterned cotton using the template provided.

- Cut two long 10cm (4 inch) wide strips from the red and white dot fabric.

sew

- For the apron front and back, sew the patterned panel to the bottom of the turquoise panels using a 1.2cm (½ inch) seam. Press the seam down, so it lies behind the patterned fabric.

- The pleats on the front and back of the apron are folded from the outside inwards. Use the positioning marks you drew along the top of each rectangle to pin the pleats and stitch them in place at either end with a short row of machine stitching 2cm (¾ inch) from the edge.

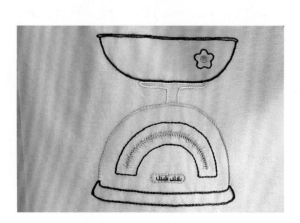

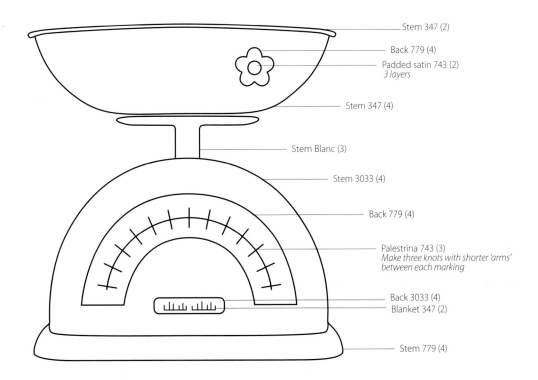

Stem 347 (2)

Back 779 (4)

Padded satin 743 (2)
3 layers

Stem 347 (4)

Stem Blanc (3)

Stem 3033 (4)

Back 779 (4)

Palestrina 743 (3)
*Make three knots with shorter 'arms'
between each marking*

Back 3033 (4)
Blanket 347 (2)

Stem 779 (4)

- Line up the apron front and back, wrong sides facing. Match up the pleats and seams where the patterned and plain fabric meets. Pin, then bind the sides and bottom edges together with the red binding.

- To create the band and apron ties, cut one of the strips of red and white dot fabric in half and join a piece to either end of the remaining strip with a 0.6cm (¼ inch) seam, then press the seams open. Joining the fabric in this way creates symmetry in the ties and prevents the joins from appearing in the centre of the apron.

- Fold the short ends in by 1.2cm (½ inch) and stitch in place.

- Fold the strip in half lengthways and iron the fold in place. Open it out again and then fold the edges in to meet the centre fold; iron these new folds in place, too, as you would to make binding.

- Find the halfway point, measure 89cm (35 inches) either way and cut to get a 178cm (70 inch) strip of fabric.

- Match up the halfway point of the ties with the centre point of the apron and pin in place, folding over the top of the apron.

- Sew along the edge from one end of the strip to the other, closing the ties and attaching the band to the top of the apron in one go.

Pineapple

There are many ways to break up a pineapple into segments, but arced lines create the perfect spaces for partial blanket stitch pinwheels, which themselves best resemble the fruit's spiky surface.

Thread

DMC six-stranded cotton thread:

- 726 Light topaz
- 779 Dark cocoa
- 3345 Dark hunter green

Needles

- Embroidery: size 7, 9

Enlarge by 300%

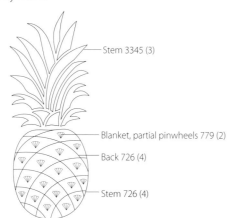

- Stem 3345 (3)
- Blanket, partial pinwheels 779 (2)
- Back 726 (4)
- Stem 726 (4)

Sailboat

A vintage chapter would be incomplete without a nod to cross stitch. The stitch placement of this design is adapted to work for surface embroidery in that the individual cross stitches are isolated rather than joined.

Thread

DMC six-stranded cotton thread:

- B5200 Snow white
- 3847 Dark teal green
- 3848 Medium teal green

Needles

- Embroidery: size 7

Enlarge by 250%

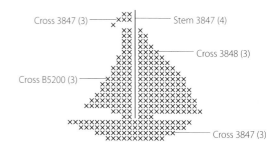

- Cross 3847 (3)
- Stem 3847 (4)
- Cross 3848 (3)
- Cross B5200 (3)
- Cross 3847 (3)

SKILL LEVEL ⨯⨯

SKILL LEVEL ⨯⨯⨯

Flamingo

Begin the beak with the black tip and angle your stitches downwards. Embroider the top and bottom halves by starting near the eye and adjust the angle of your stitches as you get nearer the tip. Stitch the row down the centre of the beak last.

Ice cream cone

A couched trellis creates the diamond pattern typically found on ice-cream cones, while a back stitch trellis depicts the embossed squares that give wafers their distinctive look.

Thread

DMC six-stranded cotton thread:

- 310 Black
- B5200 Snow white
- 3706 Medium melon
- 168 Very light pewter

- 3705 Dark melon
- 3801 Very dark melon

Needles

- Embroidery: size 7, 9

Thread

DMC six-stranded cotton thread:

- 727 Very light topaz
- B5200 Snow white
- 3811 Very light turquoise
- 955 Light Nile green
- 3713 Very light salmon

- 3712 Medium salmon
- 3033 Very light mocha brown

Needles

- Embroidery: size 7, 9

Enlarge by 300%

Satin B5200 (2) — Satin 168 (1)
Satin 310 (2) — Back 310 (1)
Embroider over satin stitching
Satin 3706 (2) — Stem 3705 (4)

Back 3706 (4)

Satin 3801 (2)

Rhodes, circular 168 (2)

Stem 168 (3)

Satin 168 (2)

Enlarge by 300%

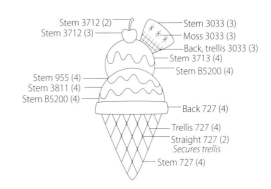

Stem 3712 (2) — Stem 3033 (3)
Stem 3712 (3) — Moss 3033 (3)
Back, trellis 3033 (3)
Stem 3713 (4)
Stem B5200 (4)
Stem 955 (4)
Stem 3811 (4)
Stem B5200 (4)
Back 727 (4)
Trellis 727 (4)
Straight 727 (2)
Secures trellis
Stem 727 (4)

festive

*Seasonal décor gets a personal touch
with hand stitching*

Fair Isle reindeer runner

A HINT OF KNITTING FOR YOUR CHRISTMAS TABLE

The classic red on white embroidery on the table runner can easily be swapped for colours that match your festive décor, and incorporating metallic threads – whipping the chain stitch in sparkling silver, for example – would add a whole new element to the design. Equally, you could choose to use a multitude of thread colours for a bright and cheerful version.

The measurements given here are for a runner to fit a 160 x 90cm (63 x 35 inch) table. To adjust it to fit your dining table, measure the length and add 25–30cm (10–12 inches) to each end for the overhang. Think about where you'd like your embroidery to appear as well: towards the ends so it hangs off the edge of the table or further in so it lies on top of your table? It's really down to personal taste.

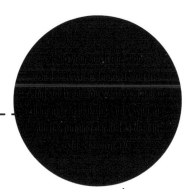

Fabric
- 2.2m (87 inches) white cotton
- 50cm (20 inches) cotton voile backing fabric

Thread
DMC six-stranded cotton thread:
- 347 Very dark salmon
- B5200 Snow white

Needles
- Embroidery: size 7, 9
- Milliner: size 7

Other
- 6m (19¾ feet) white piping
- Matching sewing thread

Embroidery design
Enlarge by 200%

prepare

- Cut the white cotton in half lengthways. Draw a 213 x 45.5cm (84 x 18 inch) rectangle on one half, with positioning marks on either side at 35cm (14 inches), 60cm (24 inches), 142cm (56 inches) and 168cm (66 inches). Cut two 23 x 50cm (9 x 20 inch) pieces of voile.

transfer

- Transfer the embroidery design facing outwards at either end of the fabric, using one of the methods given on page 17. Position the design between the marks on the cutting lines. Tack a piece of cotton voile behind each design.

embroider

- Embroider the design according to the instructions.
- When the embroidery is complete, place the fabric face down on a towel and iron it from the back. Iron the rest of the runner, avoiding the embroidered sections, before sewing.

cut

- Check that the drawn-on cutting lines haven't distorted during stitching and redraw them if necessary before cutting out the runner.
- Use the front as a template and cut the back of the runner out of the other half of the cotton fabric.

sew

- Stitch the piping around the edges of the front of the runner, lining up the raw edges and stitching as close to the piping as possible. Use your sewing machine's zipper foot if you're using thicker piping.
- Pin the runner front to the back, right sides facing, and use the piping stitching as a guide (sew over it) to join the front and back. Leave a gap at one end for turning.
- Trim the corners, turn the right way round and push the corners out neatly with a closed pair of scissors.
- Stitch the gap closed by hand with small, invisible stitches.
- Press the seams gently to avoid squashing the piping.

Satin 347 (2)

French knots 347 (2)

Arrowhead 347 (3)

Whipped chain 347 (3) +
B5200 (2)

Chinese knots 347 (2)

Fly 347 (3)
Start with a straight stitch

Four-legged knots 347 (3)

Star 347 (2)
*Omit the last, securing
stitch*

French knots 347 (2)

Stem 347 (4)

Consistency is key in this
design – try and keep your knots
and isolated stitches as evenly
spaced and lined up
as possible.

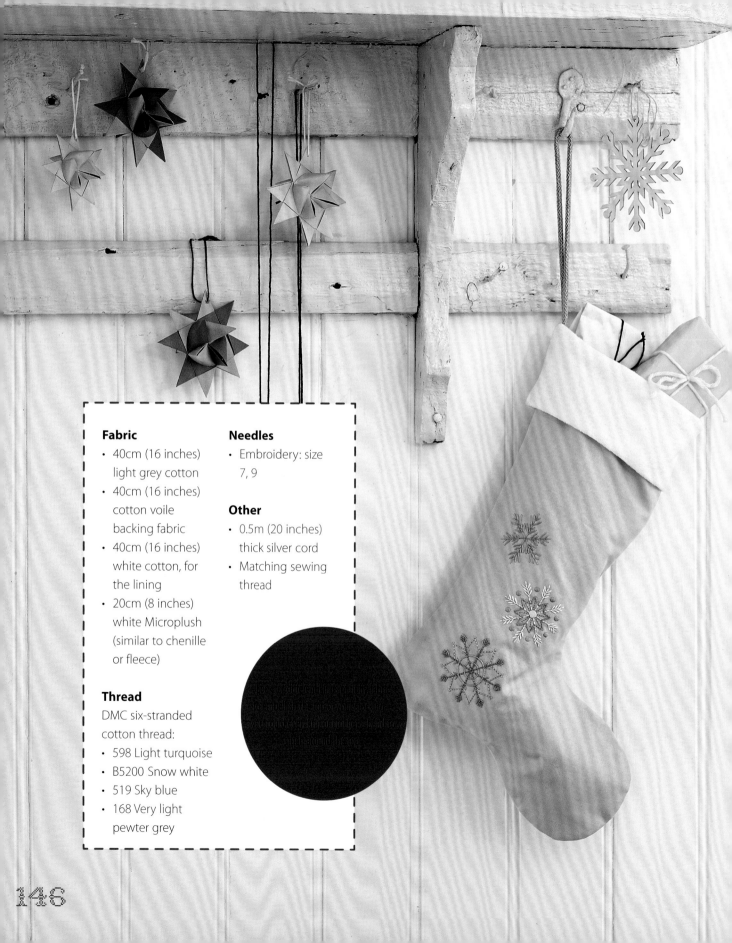

Fabric

- 40cm (16 inches) light grey cotton
- 40cm (16 inches) cotton voile backing fabric
- 40cm (16 inches) white cotton, for the lining
- 20cm (8 inches) white Microplush (similar to chenille or fleece)

Thread

DMC six-stranded cotton thread:

- 598 Light turquoise
- B5200 Snow white
- 519 Sky blue
- 168 Very light pewter grey

Needles

- Embroidery: size 7, 9

Other

- 0.5m (20 inches) thick silver cord
- Matching sewing thread

Snowflake stocking

A SNOWY SCENE FOR THE MANTELPIECE

Fly stitch is highly effective when embroidering snowflakes, especially when combined with back stitch and arranged in a spiral. The top snowflake is embroidered entirely in these two stitches – give or take a straight stitch or two.

Personalise a stocking for each family member by embroidering it in their favourite colours and using different fabrics for the body and folded-over top. If you prefer coordinated stockings hanging from the mantelpiece, use different hanging cords to distinguish them from each other.

prepare

- Cut the grey fabric in half so you have a 40 x 50cm (16 x 20 inch) piece for the front of the stocking. Cut a 40 x 50cm (16 x 20 inch) piece of cotton voile.

transfer

- Transfer the stocking design onto one of the pieces of grey fabric using one of the methods given on page 17, including the cutting lines. Overlock or tack the cotton voile to the back.

embroider

- Embroider the design according to the instructions.
- Iron the completed embroidery face down on a towel, from the back.

cut

- Check that the traced-on cutting lines haven't distorted during stitching and redraw them if necessary before cutting out the stocking front.
- Use the front as a template and cut another stocking shape from the grey fabric, plus another two from the white cotton for the lining.
- Fold the Microplush in half, right sides facing, and use the template provided to cut out the top.
- Cut a 38cm (15 inch) length of silver cord.

sew

- Place the two grey stocking pieces face to face, and the two pieces of lining face to face. Then lay the grey stocking shapes on top of the linings with the embroidered panel on top and pin all the pieces together. Layering them in this way will hide the seam when the stocking is turned the right way round.
- Join the layers using a 0.6cm (¼ inch) seam. Leave the top, straight edge of the stocking open.

Templates, embroidery instructions and design
Enlarge by 300%

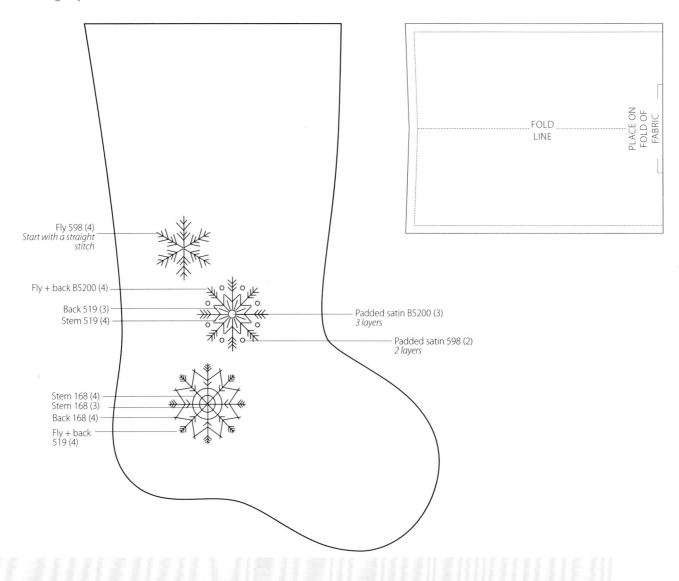

Fly 598 (4)
Start with a straight stitch

Fly + back B5200 (4)

Back 519 (3)
Stem 519 (4)

Padded satin B5200 (3)
3 layers

Padded satin 598 (2)
2 layers

Stem 168 (4)
Stem 168 (3)
Back 168 (4)
Fly + back 519 (4)

FOLD LINE

PLACE ON FOLD OF FABRIC

- Turn the stocking the right way round through the top opening and press the seams gently.

- Sew the stocking top into a tube by joining the two short sides. Use a 0.6cm (¼ inch) seam.

- Fold the stocking top in half lengthways with the right side of the fabric facing outwards.

- Slip it into the top of the stocking and line up the edges with the raw edges of the stocking.

- Fold the cord in half to form a loop and slide it into the back of the stocking, between the stocking top and the grey fabric, so the ends stick up between the layers.

- Stitch around the top, joining all the layers and securing the cord, using a 0.6cm (¼ inch) seam. Overlock or zigzag the raw edge.

- Fold the top back over the stocking. The hanging cord should now be visible. Gently press the seam if necessary.

Star garland

A STRING OF STARS TO ADD FESTIVE CHEER

The embroidery is the quick part of this project, putting the stars together takes a little longer. But it's a fun project for lovers of hand sewing.

The stars are assembled using the English paper-piecing quilting technique, with stiffening rather than paper – and it stays put to help maintain the shape of the stars. Folding the fabric behind the sharp points is a little fiddly, but it becomes easier once you get a bit of a rhythm going.

Fabric
- 30cm (12 inches) white cotton
- 30cm (12 inches) white cotton voile backing fabric
- 20cm (8 inches) red patterned cotton
- 20cm (8 inches) blue patterned cotton
- 20cm (8 inches) green patterned cotton
- 20cm (8 inches) blue and white dot cotton
- 20cm (8 inches) black and white chevron cotton

Thread
DMC six-stranded cotton thread:
- 351 Coral
- 350 Medium coral
- 989 Forest green
- 598 Light turquoise
- 744 Pale yellow
- 165 Very light moss green
- 519 Sky blue

Needles
- Embroidery: size 7

Other
- 3m (9 feet 10 inches) cord
- Quilters' batting
- Cardstock
- Sewing thread
- 0.5m (20 inches) thick, iron-on stiffening (Vilene)

FABRIC TEMPLATES (FROM CENTRE OUTWARDS)
1. Stiffening small star (cut 2)
2. Fabric small star (cut 2)
3. Stiffening medium star (cut 2)
4. Stiffening embroidered star (cut 2)
5. Fabric medium star (cut 2)
6. Fabric embroidered star back (cut 1)

You can adjust the length of the garland by adding or removing stars, or spacing them differently. This one's about 2.5m (8.2 feet) long

BATTING
SMALL STAR
CUT 2 OF EACH

BATTING
MEDIUM STAR
CUT 2 OF EACH

BATTING
EMBROIDERED
STAR
CUT 2 OF EACH

Embroidery instructions and designs
Enlarge by 300%

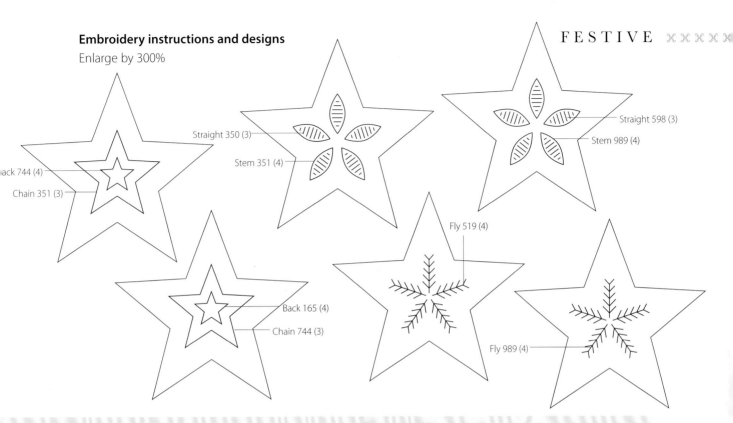

Straight 350 (3)

Stem 351 (4)

Straight 598 (3)

Stem 989 (4)

ack 744 (4)

Chain 351 (3)

Back 165 (4)

Chain 744 (3)

Fly 519 (4)

Fly 989 (4)

prepare
- Cut the white cotton into six pieces and make templates for each of the star shapes out of card, to trace around.

transfer
- Transfer a star design (two of each) onto each piece of fabric using one of the methods given on page 17. Include the cutting lines. Overlock or tack a piece of voile to the back of each.

embroider
- Embroider the design according to the instructions and iron face down on a towel.

cut
- Cut the embroidered stars out along the traced on cutting lines.
- Cut a backing for each embroidered star from the various patterned fabrics.
- Cut enough patterned star shapes to make four medium and six small stars.

- Cut out a stiffening star for each fabric star shape.
- Cut batting stars to pad six embroidered, four medium and six small stars.

sew
- Centre a corresponding stiffening shape on the back of each fabric star and fuse it in place with a hot iron. For the embroidered stars, iron face down on a towel so the stitching sinks in and isn't pressed flat.
- Fold in the fabric edges of each star and tack in place – the edge of the stiffening is your fold line. Snip the fabric at the base of each point to allow it to splay. Start along a straight side and at the points, fold your fabric three times to fit the excess behind the stiffening, starting with a horizontal fold over the point.
- Layer each star with the corresponding batting sandwiched between the fabric back and front, with the smallest batting stars in the centre.
- Tie a hanging loop in one end of the cord and begin attaching the stars, with the cord running through the centres. Oversew the front of each star to its back with sewing thread, then remove the tacking.
- When finished, trim your cord and tie another hanging loop.

Holly cutlery holder

ROOMY ENOUGH TO BE STOCKED UP FOR MAINS AND DESSERT

Small bullion knots add to the texture of the design, but you could also embroider the veins of the holly leaves in long-armed feather stitch. Back stitch is a good choice for spiky leaves as it lends itself well to sharp points, making for easier stitching.

Make as many as you need for your table, change the thread colours for a mix and match look or stick with white for more classic table décor. The cutlery holder is big enough for a knife, fork and that all-important pudding spoon.

Stitch a piece of piping along the top edge of the holder for a classy touch and to make them slightly more formal.

Fabric
- 45 x 15cm (18 x 6 inches) silver-grey cotton
- 45 x 15cm (18 x 6 inches) cotton voile backing fabric
- 45 x 15cm (18 x 6 inches) white cotton

Thread
DMC six-stranded cotton thread:
- B5200 Snow white

Needles
- Embroidery: size 7, 9
- Milliner: size 8

Other
- 15cm (6 inches) thin white piping
- Matching sewing thread

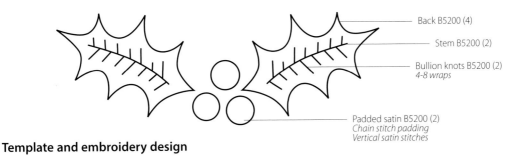

Back B5200 (4)

Stem B5200 (2)

Bullion knots B5200 (2)
4-8 wraps

Padded satin B5200 (2)
Chain stitch padding
Vertical satin stitches

Template and embroidery design

Enlarge by 250%

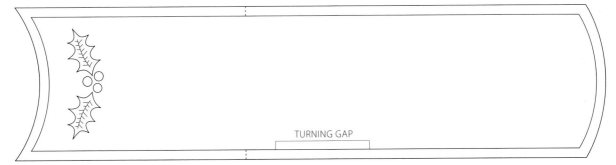

TURNING GAP

transfer

- Transfer the design onto the silver-grey cotton using one of the methods given on page 17. Include the cutting lines and fold marks. Overlock or tack the voile to the back.

embroider

- Embroider the design according to the instructions.
- Iron the embroidery with it lying face down on a towel.

cut

- Check that the traced-on cutting lines haven't distorted during stitching and redraw them if necessary before cutting out the holder.

sew

- Machine stitch the piping to the top curved edge of the embroidered panel (above the embroidery) using a 0.6cm (¼ inch) seam. Stitch as close to the piping as possible.
- Pin the holder front to the back, right sides facing, and use the piping stitching as a guide (sew over it) to join the front and back top edges. Clip the seam to allow it to splay when it is turned the right way round.
- Make one or two small tailor's tacks on the right side of the fabric alongside the fold marks so you know where to fold once the marks are hidden inside the seams.
- Stitch around the rest of the holder, leaving a gap where indicated for turning. Pivot the fabric at the corners with your needle in the down position.
- Trim the corners and turn the right way round. Press the seam and a 0.6cm (¼ inch) hem into the fabric on each side of the gap.
- Fold the holder in half using the tailor's tacks as a guide and hand sew the edges together using small invisible stitching and closing up the gap as you go. Remove the tailor's tacks.

If you want extra-round berries, pad them with chain stitch as well as a layer or two of satin stitch.

Hanging birds

FOR YOUR TREE, BALUSTRADE OR FRONT-DOOR WREATH

Fresh green and white fabric and threads give these hanging bird decorations an elegant Christmas feel. To embroider the birds on both sides, flip the pattern so you have a mirror image of the original before transferring it onto the fabric.

The birds are fairly straightforward to make, but it's easier if you tack the fabric together before sewing to eliminate the need to sew around pins.

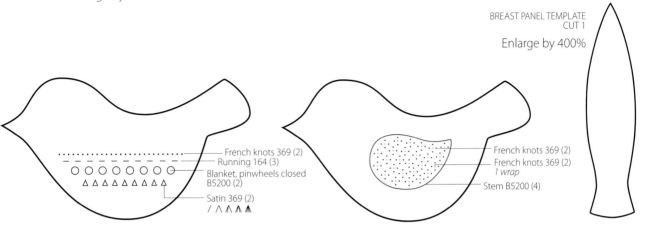

BREAST PANEL TEMPLATE
CUT 1
Enlarge by 400%

SKILL
LEVEL
✗

French knots 369 (2)
Running 164 (3)
Blanket, pinwheels closed
B5200 (2)
Satin 369 (2)

French knots 369 (2)
French knots 369 (2)
1 wrap
Stem B5200 (4)

Fabric

- 61 x 25cm (24 x 10 inches) white cotton
- 61 x 25cm (24 x 10 inches) white cotton voile backing fabric
- 30 x 25cm (12 x 10 inches) green and white dot cotton

Thread

DMC six-stranded cotton thread:

- 369 Very light pistachio green
- B5200 Snow white
- 164 Light forest green

Needles

- Embroidery: size 7, 9
- Milliner: size 8

Other

- 60cm (24 inches) cord in your chosen colour
- Stuffing
- Matching sewing thread

prepare

- Cut the white cotton fabric and the voile in half so you have two roughly square pieces of fabric, one for each bird.

transfer

- Transfer the bird designs onto the two pieces of white cotton using one of the methods given on page 17. Include the cutting lines. Overlock or tack a piece of voile to the back of each.

embroider

- Embroider the design according to the instructions.
- Iron the embroidery by placing the fabric face down on a towel and ironing the back.

cut

- Cut the birds out along the traced-on cutting lines.
- Use the embroidered panels as templates to cut out the backs of the birds – place them face down.
- Cut out two breast panels from the patterned fabric using the template provided.
- Cut the cord in half, into two 30cm (12 inch) lengths.

sew

- Loop the cord and pin to the front of each embroidered bird towards the head, with the cord hanging down over the body. Sew in place close enough to the edge of the fabric so the stitching will fall inside the seam.
- Tack each bird front to its back from the beak, going across the back and to the top of the tail, then machine stitch, securing the cord as you go. Trim the cord once stitched. Notch the fabric inside the seam allowance around the head and clip it along the curve of the back.
- Tack the breast panel to each side of the bird from the beak to the tail and machine stitch around the edges using a 0.6cm (¼ inch) seam. At the beak, stitch right up to the top seam, fasten off and then start again on the other side of the seam, as close to it as possible and in line with the end of the row of stitching you just sewed. Leave a gap along the back bottom edge for turning.
- Remove the tacking, trim the cord and then turn the bird the right way round through the gap.
- Stuff until nice and firm, but not bulging, and stitch closed by hand with small, invisible stitching.

Tree ornaments

FUN AND EASY CHRISTMAS DECORATIONS FOR YOUR TREE

Get your friends and family round for an afternoon of stitching. Quick to embroider and fun to make, these hanging decorations can be made in infinite colour and fabric variations and are bound to add cheer to any festive tree. Match the fabric to your thread colours and make extras out of two contrasting fabrics to fill in the gaps.

The decorations are a no-sew project as they're embroidered rather than sewn together. And the adaption of an appliqué technique ensures the two halves end up perfectly round.

Fabric
- 20cm (8 inches) white cotton
- 20cm (8 inches) cotton voile backing fabric
- 20cm (8 inch) squares of patterned cotton in five different colours

Thread
DMC six-stranded cotton thread:

Angel (✕✕)
- 369 Very light pistachio green
- 519 Sky blue
- B5200 Snow white
- 168 Very light pewter grey
- 744 Pale yellow

Bauble (✕)
- 164 Light forest green
- 519 Sky blue
- 3328 Dark salmon
- 744 Pale yellow

Candy cane (✕✕)
- B5200 Snow white
- 347 Very dark salmon

Gingerbread man (✕✕)
- B5200 Snow white
- 435 Very light brown
- 744 Pale yellow
- 434 Light brown

Tree (✕)
- 989 Forest green
- 347 Very dark salmon

Use black and white cord for the hanging loops to give the ornaments a contemporary feel.

Needles
- Embroidery: size 7, 9
- Milliner: 7

Other
- Quilters' batting/ wadding
- 1m (40 inches) black and white cord
- Matching sewing threads
- Cardstock

prepare

- Cut a 20x20cm (8 x 8 inch) square of white cotton and cotton voile for each decoration. Draw a circle measuring 11.5cm (4½ inches) in diameter on each piece of fabric.

transfer

- Centre an embroidery design inside each of the drawn on circles and transfer using one of the methods given on page 17. Overlock or tack the cotton voile to the back.

embroider

- Embroider the designs according to the instructions and iron face down on a towel when complete.

cut

- Cut out each of the decorations along the circular, drawn-on cutting line.
- Cut a circle the same size from each of the patterned fabrics.
- For each ornament, cut two sets of five circles of batting measuring 8.25cm (3¼ inches), 7cm (2¾ inches), 5.5cm (2¼ inches) 5cm (2 inches) in diameter.
- Cut two circles of cardstock for each decoration, measuring 8.25cm (3¼ inches) in diameter.
- Cut a 25cm (10 inch) length of cord for each decoration.

sew

- Layer the five circles of batting in size order. Place a circle of card on top of the stack, with the smallest circle of batting lying against the card. This creates a dome shape.
- Tack around the edge of the embroidered fabric circle, leaving tails of thread at either end.
- Turn the fabric upside down and centre the stack of batting and card on top of the fabric. Pull the ends of the tacking thread to gather the fabric around the card. Pull until the fabric is lying snugly against the card and then knot the thread.
- Repeat for the patterned fabric circle.
- Fold the cord in half to create a hanging loop and tape the two loose ends to the card at the back of one of the circles, leaving a 15cm (6 inch) loop sticking out.
- Sandwich the fabric circles back to back with the loop between them.
- Stitch the circles together with Palestrina stitch, using six strands of 519 for the angel, 347 for the candy cane, 989 for the tree, 164 for the bauble and 744 for the gingerbread man.
- Using matching sewing thread, cobble the hanging cord to either side of each decoration by hand to secure it.

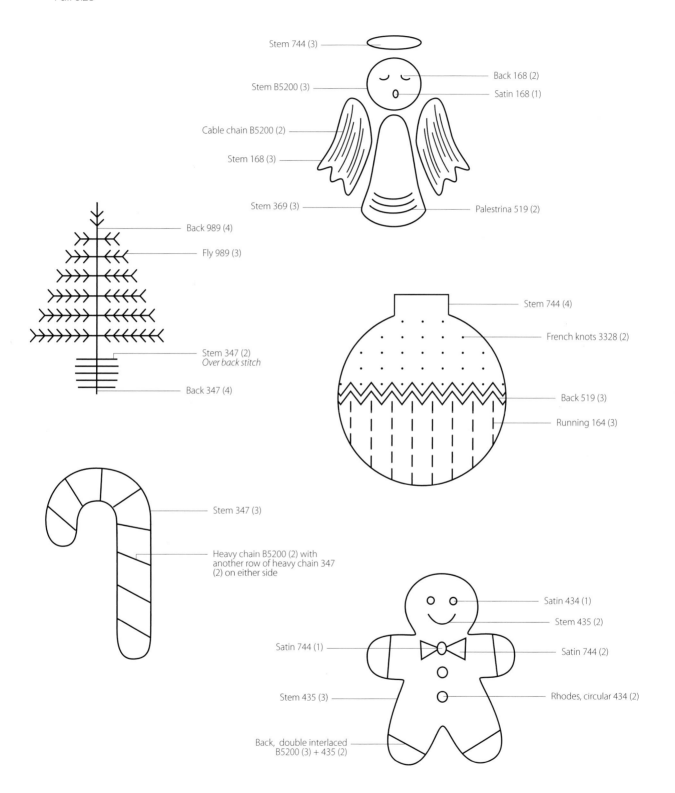

Stem 744 (3)

Back 168 (2)

Stem B5200 (3)

Satin 168 (1)

Cable chain B5200 (2)

Stem 168 (3)

Stem 369 (3)

Palestrina 519 (2)

Back 989 (4)

Fly 989 (3)

Stem 347 (2)
Over back stitch

Back 347 (4)

Stem 744 (4)

French knots 3328 (2)

Back 519 (3)

Running 164 (3)

Stem 347 (3)

Heavy chain B5200 (2) with
another row of heavy chain 347
(2) on either side

Satin 434 (1)

Stem 435 (2)

Satin 744 (1)

Satin 744 (2)

Stem 435 (3)

Rhodes, circular 434 (2)

Back, double interlaced
B5200 (3) + 435 (2)

Acknowledgements

When Judith Hannam first approached me to do this book, she couldn't have known how well-timed that first email was or how ready I was to take on a project like this. Communication with Kyle Cathie followed and I'm grateful for her easygoing manner and willingness to answer questions. My editor, Tara O'Sullivan, made it effortless to work together on a project with an ocean between us and guided me through the process of designing and writing a book with ease. Many thanks must go to photographer Vanessa Davies and stylist Polly Webb-Wilson (I'm only sorry we couldn't fit in more of their beautiful photographs). Thanks also to Kuo Kang Cheng for illustrating the stitches in such a clear and visually enticing way, and to Heidi Baker for the fresh and contemporary design of the book. Helena Caldon and Lisa Pinnell edited the copy and dealt with production respectively, thank you. Thanks also to the team at Kyle Books for the constant feedback – it was an added bonus getting so many professional opinions on my work. Lastly, a huge thank you to Barbara Skinner for her hours and hours of help. She not only embroidered many of the projects in this book, she also made and hand quilted the leaf throw and was a sounding board throughout the months it took to create this book.

First published in Great Britain in 2015 by
Kyle Books, an imprint of Kyle Cathie Ltd
192–198 Vauxhall Bridge Road
London SW1V 1DX
general.enquiries@kylebooks.com
www.kylebooks.com

10 9 8 7 6 5 4 3 2 1
ISBN 978 0 85783 297 9

Text © 2015 Kelly Fletcher
Design © 2015 Kyle Books
Photographs © 2015 Vanessa Davies*
Illustrations © Kuo Kang Chen
* Except page 129, © 2015 Kelly Fletcher

Project Editor: Tara O'Sullivan
Copy Editor: Helena Caldon
Designer: Heidi Baker
Photographer: Vanessa Davies
Illustrator: Kuo Kang Chen
Prop Stylist: Polly Webb-Wilson

Production: Lisa Pinnell

A Cataloguing in Publication record for this title is available from the British Library.

Colour reproduction by Alta London
Printed and bound in China by C&C Offset Printing Co., Ltd.